This Vast External Realm: Essays of Dean Acheson

Among Friends: Personal Letters of Dean Acheson
(with David S. McLellan)

Acheson
Country

Acheson
Country

A Memoir

DAVID C. ACHESON

W·W·NORTON & COMPANY

NEW YORK · LONDON

FRONTISPIECE PHOTOGRAPH: *Alice and Dean Acheson at Harewood Farm, 1950s.*

F I R S T   E D I T I O N

The text of this book is composed in Avanta with the display typeset in Cactus. Composition and manufacturing by The Haddon Craftsmen. Book design by Marjorie J. Flock.

Library of Congress Cataloging-in-Publication Data

Acheson, David C.
  Acheson country: a memoir / David C. Acheson.
     p.   cm.
  1. Acheson, Dean, 1893–1971.   2. Statesmen—United States-
-Biography.   3. Acheson, David C.   I. Title.
E748.A15A597   1993
973.7′092—dc20   92-40856

ISBN 0-393-03530-1

W. W. Norton & Company, Inc., 500 Fifth Avenue, New York, N.Y. 10110
W. W. Norton & Company Ltd., 10 Coptic Street, London WC1A 1PU

1 2 3 4 5 6 7 8 9 0

To Pat, Eldie, David, and Peter

Contents

9

Contents

Foreword

THE PURPOSE of this book is quite specific. It does not purport to be a broad personal memoir. Rather, it seeks to knit together pieces and vignettes to make up a personal character portrait of my father, Dean Acheson. Though treated well by contemporary history, he has come through to the reading public as the author and symbol of a foreign policy, but not vividly as a human being. Accordingly, I have sought to present in this book a series of snapshots of his personality so that a three-dimensional individual can emerge.

I have used, so far as possible, remembered episodes, stories, historical background, so that the portraiture is worked by the events themselves rather than by me. All this is chiefly from my own personal recollection.

My father always believed that a good story does not have to be an affidavit, that is, the juice of entertainment should not be squeezed out by fanatically literal accuracy. While this is my own inclination also, there is here only an occasional finial or embellishment.

These vignettes tell of an arresting personality, depicted at different times and places and in circumstances influenced by territory, fellow residents, and disparate activities. The interaction of the personality and the encompassing environment suggested a title that would comprehend both, hence *Acheson Country.*

David C. Acheson

October 1992

Acknowledgments

M Y THANKS go to my wife and children and to a number of friends, particularly Luke Battle, Peter Walker, and Joe and Rhonda Johnston, without whose encouragement I might not have persisted with this writing. Peg and Gerry Gesell were most forthcoming in providing helpful material.

I am grateful to Eloise Marker who did the word processing on some early chapters and to Terri Edwards who did the same on the bulk of the text. They put up with my handwriting and my endless guests for *le mot juste.*

Special thanks go to Patricia Hass, whose encouragement and wise and knowledgeable advice helped me turn an idea into a book.

I am very grateful to David McCullough, who generously read the typescript, made many astute suggestions, and provided the Introduction.

NOTE

The following titles are abbreviated in the footnotes to the text:

Among Friends   *Among Friends: Personal Letters of Dean Acheson,* edited by David S. McLellan and David C. Acheson. (New York: Dodd, Mead, 1980).

Morning and Noon   *Morning and Noon, A Memoir,* by Dean Acheson (Boston: Houghton Mifflin, 1965).

Present at the Creation   *Present at the Creation: My Years in the State Department,* by Dean Acheson (New York: W. W. Norton & Company, 1969).

Introduction
by David McCullough

I SAW MY FIRST AUTHENTIC, flesh-and-blood personage of history—my first Great Man on the hoof, as it were—on a morning in New Haven, Connecticut, in the fall of 1953. Or maybe 1954. I was a Yale undergraduate on my way to class, heading along York Street, alone and wrapped in my own private undergraduate fog, when all at once, at the corner where the high-priced clothing stores were concentrated, out from the door of J. Press, stepped Dean Acheson.

There was no mistaking him. He couldn't have been more conspicuous. Or I more astonished. There had been nothing in the papers about his being on campus, no talk of it that I had heard. Yet there he was not thirty feet ahead, the former Secretary of State, member of the Yale Corporation, Class of 1915, surely the most famous living Yale graduate of the day. Besides, for many of us he was something of a hero, for the way he had faced the attacks of Senator Joe McCarthy.

It wasn't just that he looked bigger than life but that he seemed, poised there on York Street, in drab New Haven, almost to be overdoing the whole responsibility of being Dean Acheson—the spectacular tailoring, the mustache, the lift of the chin. It was as though some splendid actor in perfect Acheson dress had stepped suddenly from the wings and I was his only audience.

I'm tempted to say he even consulted his watch with suitably theatrical flourish, but that would be stretching it.

Being alone, I had no one with whom to compare notes later. Nor, I'm sorry to say, had I the temerity to approach such an apparition or exchange a greeting before he walked off—strode off—straight as a drum major, round the corner on what I could only imagine as business of the highest priority.

Once seen, he was not to be forgotten. Without a word, with manner and appearance only, he seemed to say, "I am no ordinary man and these, sir, are no ordinary times." And while my chance encounter had invigorated the morning in a way I never before experienced, it was also a little humbling. For if here, in this glorious figure, was the ultimate Yale man, the grandest of old Blues, what chance was there for a member of the Class of 1955 ever to measure up?

. . . How I wish now that I had said something, said hello, said anything, now that I know so much more about him and the part he played in shaping our times. As Assistant Secretary and Under Secretary of State during Harry Truman's first years in office, Acheson was a driving force in the creation of the Truman Doctrine and the Marshall Plan. As Secretary of State from January 1949 to January 1953, through all four years of Truman's second term, it was Acheson who was largely responsible for the establishment of NATO and for the decision to proceed with the development of the hydrogen bomb. It was he who orchestrated the tense, crucial days in June 1950, one emergency meeting after another at Blair House, that led to

Truman's most difficult of all decisions, to enter the Korean War; he, with Secretary of Defense George Marshall and the Joint Chiefs, who stood with Truman in the brave, incendiary decision to sack General MacArthur.

Truman considered the position of Secretary of State second only to the President. He believed in a strong Secretary and chose for the job three extremely strong figures, James Byrnes, Marshall, and Acheson. But it was the lordly, controversial Acheson who proved the strongest, most brilliant of them all.

For Truman, importantly, Acheson was also something more—friend, confidant, intimate correspondent. His place in Truman's official family and in Truman's heart was unrivaled, for all the surface differences between them. That Harry Truman of Independence, Missouri, Truman the one-time dirt farmer, Truman the failed haberdasher and former pal of Boss Tom Pendergast, that plain Harry, known for his impatience with "high hats," who loathed pretense and judged people by what they were rather than by where they came from, or the schools they attended, or the clothes they wore, saw such value in Acheson right from the start, demonstrates as clearly as almost anything can how much more there was to Acheson, as to Truman, than met the eye.

Once, at one of the very lowest points in Truman's fortunes as President, in 1946, when the Republicans swept the off-year elections to regain control of Congress and Truman arrived back in Washington by train, after voting in Missouri, Acheson was the only member of the entire administration who was waiting at Union Station to welcome him. Acheson went because he thought it only proper and fitting that he be there, and assuming that others would feel the same. For Truman it was a gesture he would never forget.

They were much alike, these two, in their exceptionally high conception of the presidency, and in their courage and moral stamina. Both had great physical vitality, humor, a strong sense of personal loyalty, and native, penetrating shrewdness. Each was a devoted husband and father, and they had complete trust in one another.

Their correspondence, particularly during the later years, when Truman had returned to Independence and Acheson to his Washington law practice, is one of the richest, most revealing of all the collections in the Truman Library. Acheson's letters especially, like his Pulitzer Prize-winning memoir of the Truman presidency, *Present at the Creation*, show him to be, along with everything else, a wonderfully gifted writer.

But now, in David Acheson's delightful memoir, the private, domestic Dean Acheson emerges as never before. This is a warm, intelligent, often highly entertaining portrait, a book full of interest and pleasures about a man who could hold our attention had he never figured in history, never become this century's outstanding Secretary of State. Reading it, savoring much of a family way of life now largely vanished from the American scene, makes me treasure even more the memory of the man I saw one day on York Street.

Acheson
Country

Palladio in Georgetown; garden of Acheson residence.

Early Days in
Georgetown

I N 1922, A YEAR AFTER my birth and two years before the
Teapot Dome scandal, my parents bought an old brick
house in Georgetown, at 2805 P Street (Northwest
quadrant of the District of Columbia). It had a side yard and
backyard, and a mulberry tree that towered over the side yard
and showered its unwelcome fruit over the lawn. The purchase
price, as I recall, was $24,000, which seems cheap, but incomes
were in four figures. Previously we had lived in a rented house
on Corcoran Street, a pleasant dead end off 18th Street in a
comfortably shabby part of town not far from Dupont Circle.

Georgetown was far from chic in the 1920s. Affluent people, or those wishing to make a statement, lived in the
Kalorama neighborhood, or on Massachusetts Avenue, or in
Massachusetts Avenue Park, or on Woodland Drive. The area
now called Woodley Park was then the estate of Henry L.
Stimson, who had bought it for the stables and riding when he
came to Washington as President Taft's Secretary of War.

In the block immediately east of ours on P Street, most of
the residents were black (or "colored" in the terminology of the
time), though white purchasers were increasing. Neighborhood

relations between the races were entirely civil and cooperative.

Georgetown had been a port town on the Potomac River long before the creation of the City of Washington and the District of Columbia. One saw little in the Georgetown of the 1920s, or even the 1930s, similar to the elegant restorations and modernizations that one sees today. Only a few grand houses stood out: Evermay, the residence of Lammot duPont Belin; Tudor Place, the residence for 150 years of Armistead Peter and his ancestors; Dumbarton Oaks, once the residence of Vice President John C. Calhoun and, at the time of this narrative, of Robert Woods Bliss, an ambassador and a great seigneur of Georgetown. His wife gave musicales at Dumbarton Oaks; she was an heiress of the fortune made by the children's tonic, Fletcher's Castoria ("Children cry for it"). Both the Blisses were people of elevated taste and artistic sense.

There is a story about Robert Bliss and Dumbarton Oaks that I dare not vouch for, but others have. At the time of the 1932 election, Bliss was serving under President Hoover as ambassador to Argentina. He sent Franklin Roosevelt, a personal friend, a letter of congratulations on the election results, adding, in jest, "You will soon receive my *pro forma* letter of resignation," referring to the tradition that all presidential appointees tender their resignations to a new president. In due course, he tendered his resignation—and it was accepted. At that time, Robert and Mildred Bliss had cross wills leaving Dumbarton Oaks to the United States to be the residence of the Vice President (in keeping with the Calhoun precedent). The Blisses returned home via New York, stopped at their lawyers, and changed their wills to leave Dumbarton Oaks to Harvard University, which owns it still.

At the corner one block north on 28th Street from our house was a large, handsome white stucco house, the residence of Senator Medill McCormick of Illinois and his able and highly political wife, Ruth Hanna McCormick. Their daughter, "Bazy," later publisher of the *Washington Times Herald* (a morning daily still later bought by *The Washington Post*) was my frequent playmate in these early years, an intelligent and adventurous girl who would test one's nerve in "follow the leader" by walking the tops of walls and fence rails.

Georgetown was simpler in those days. It was a real neighborhood. Neighbors knew each other, spoke frequently, and did favors for each other. There were convenience stores where proprietor and customer had a personal acquaintance. A trolley-car line ran west straight out P Street from Dupont Circle to Wisconsin Avenue, and out Wisconsin Avenue to the Friendship car barn, near Western Avenue, the Maryland state line. In the fair season, the trolley was an open car (no sides or windows to the seats), and the great recreation for us children was to coax Dad to ride the open trolley with us to the Friendship stop. The conductor was no match for an active child who could hop off the rear of the open car before the fare collector got to him, then run ahead and jump on the front. Dad explained to us that this practice was dishonest and unethical, and if everyone did it the trolley would collect no fares and would have to terminate service, etc., but these consequences seemed remote.

Our house on P Street had an unusual historic feature that made it quite a conversation piece. The narrow brick apron between the house and the steps down to the sidewalk was bounded by an iron fence of heavy, black palings. Close inspection revealed that they were tapered, and a small iron knob appeared at the narrow end. The fact was that the fence was made of musket barrels from the Mexican War, and the knob was the sight at the end of the barrel. Years later, in World War II, Secretary of the Interior Harold Ickes read a press account of the musket-barrel fence and offered to send his operatives to take the fence in for the scrap drive. Dad advised him that anyone who came to take the fence away would not leave under his own power. The redoubtable curmudgeon, Ickes, let the matter drop.

Our family consisted of five: Dad, Mother, my sister Jane (older than I by approximately three years), myself, and my sister Mary (younger by about three years). Dad was transplanted to Washington from his home in Middletown, Connecticut, by employment as the law clerk (in those days called "secretary") to Justice Louis D. Brandeis of the Supreme Court of the United States. Mother, a native of Detroit, Michigan, was a graduate of Wellesley College, and an artist. We three children had come in what have been called Anglo-Saxon Protestant intervals.

In these early days, prior to their purchase of a Maryland farm in 1924, my parents took a summer rental at Bluemont, Virginia, some distance northwest of Middleburg. Dad stayed at the Washington house during the week and came out for the weekend to the Bluemont road off Route 50 by open trolley, a distance of thirty-odd miles and about two hours' ride on the trolley, plus the drive from Route 50 to Bluemont. The Bluemont experience may well have been the seed that flowered into my parents' love of country living.

From my very earliest memories, Dad liked to walk. When

he got up in the morning in Georgetown he took a walk around the block with one or more of the children, usually a flying walk, with his long legs reaching out a full yard and our short legs scampering after him. He was a "strenuous life" advocate, and thought a brisk walk stirred the circulation and the brain. After his breakfast he walked to his office, a distance of some fifteen blocks, often with his close friend John Sternhagen, a U.S. Tax Court judge. On weekends, if Dad did not take us to our farm in Maryland and press us into child labor, he often took us walking on the C&O Canal towpath, or out in the Blue Ridge foothills. These walks were at a fast pace and over long distances, in heat and in cold. We learned how to set a pace that ate up the miles without exhausting the hiker.

Dad always kept himself in good shape, with regular and reasonable exercise. He was a tall, handsome man, 6 feet 1 in height. In the 1920s his weight ran 150–155 pounds, give or take a few. By the time he was sixty (1953) his weight had leveled off at about 175. He was a pipe and cigarette smoker until the 1950s, then rather abruptly stopped smoking altogether. He had a strong and well-developed chest and shoulders, probably from competitive rowing at Groton School and Yale. For his height his arms were unusually long and his legs short, as I noticed when, as an adult, I took cast-off clothes from him. Sleeves always needed shortening, trousers lengthening.

Falling hair was always a concern to Dad, even though he retained most of his hair. All his life he used a redolent Frances Fox hair lotion for grooming, which lent its scent to his dressing room. His mustache was perhaps his chief vanity. As a young adult, his reddish curly hair and his reddish mustache were a match. Then his hair turned darker, then gray, then nearly white, but his mustache maintained a color life of its own, by entirely natural means. To give his mustache the necessary insouciance, he turned the ends up a bit, not in vertical spikes, like Kaiser Wilhelm II, but in a modified guardsman style. The closest match to it that I can remember was the mustache of Field Marshal Alexander in World War II. To proof the mustache ends against gravity, Dad applied a little bit of Pinaud's mustache wax a couple of times a week. This treatment exuded a mild, pleasant fragrance, like a first-class barbershop. When we children were very small, Dad once tired of his mustache and shaved it off. The result was terror, pandemonium. He was suddenly a stranger in the house; we children ran, screaming, from his embrace. In a remarkably short time the mustache returned to his face and he to our trust and affection.

Part of our family's tradition from early days in Georgetown was the Christmas carol party on Christmas Eve. So early in my life was the first of these annual affairs that I cannot recall it, but it must have been during the Coolidge presidency. This series began as a party for Georgetown friends and their children, particularly those friends who found the Christmas spirit through song. Mother was the piano accompanist. A number of the wives had clear, strong, accurate voices, and a few of Dad's friends could carry the correct tune in a passable baritone.

The carol party had two departments—the children's party and the adults' serious singing party. In our dining room in the P Street house, the table was laid out with small sandwiches, gingerbread men with raisin buttons and eyes, cake, and ice cream. Small children squealed and giggled and spread crumbs and ice cream liberally about. In our living room—the serious singing room—was a large silver bowl of eggnog, concocted by the butler, Johnson, and brought to a rich and tasty consistency, sprinkled with grated nutmeg and reinforced with bourbon whiskey—just enough bourbon to bring the singers' enthusiasm up to the mark without materially sacrificing performance.

The singing was stage-managed by Dad. In his youth, Christmas and Easter services at his father's church were accompanied by ambitious musical programs—Bach, Handel, brass orchestra, kettledrums, and full choir. To Dad, Christmas was music. He liked to plan the order of singing with dramatic purpose, a low-key start, then a few robust favorites to move the pace up, then the crescendo part of the program.

The sedate beginning fell to *Silent Night, It Came Upon a Midnight Clear, O Little Town of Bethlehem* (in which the women's voices predominated), and a few for the singing children: *The Friendly Beasts, I Saw Three Ships, Once in David's Royal City.* Then Dad slipped the group into second gear: *We Three Kings, O Come All Ye Faithful, Good King Wenceslas, While Shepherds Watched Their Flocks by Night.* Panic often reigned as solo parts were assigned by Dad to the Three Kings, the timid hiding behind the more hardy to avoid the casting director's eye. Judge Sternhagen had a firm, rich bass voice and often drew the role of Balthazar, letting his voice drop to the floor with "Sealed in the stone-cold tomb."

Toward the end of this section of the program, Dad and

the judge stopped at the eggnog bowl to prepare an acceleration into phase three. Then it was "All right, Alice, let's have *Angels We Have Heard on High.*"

Dad had a full-throated baritone and opened it up on the first repetitive hammer blows: "Angels we have heard on high, / Sweetly singing o'er the plain." He and the judge stood together, a powerful bass section, belting out the refrain: *"Glo-o-o-o-o-o-o-o-o-o-o-o-o-r-i-a, in excelsis deo."* Dad's throat was distended like a bullfrog's, his eyebrows drawn down in intense concentration. Then, beaming, "Terrific! Better than last year."

After *Angels We Have Heard on High,* it was downhill. But one more major effort was *Minuit Chrétien,* or *O Holy Night* (in English). That carol calls for operatic range, and while Dad made a brave start, the last two lines are a good octave above the top of his range. This was where the women came into their own, as Dad slipped off center stage and sidled over to the eggnog, planning the next order of song that would work once more up to the crashing refrain, *"in excelsis deo."*

The Old World

P EOPLE OF ONE GENERATION who have not experienced the world of an older generation fail to take adequate account of the profound effect of another time in "bending the twig" which becomes the tree. It is therefore important to show something of the generation by which Dad was formed in order to understand what he was.

Early Achesons lived in and near Edinburgh, Scotland, likely acquiring the "son" suffix from partly Norse ancestry. Some of Scotland in the thirteenth, fourteenth, and fifteenth centuries was a vassal dependency of the King of Norway, as students of Prince Henry Sinclair of the Orkney Isles will know. In the late sixteenth century certain Achesons kept a country house, Gosford House, outside Edinburgh and built two houses side by side in Edinburgh on the Royal Mile (running from Holyrood to Edinburgh Castle). They stand there, in restored form, today, with our family crest on the gate; one is now the Earl Haig Museum, the other the Scottish Craft Union. As family oral history has it, one such Acheson, Sir Archibald, rendered important services to King James VI of

Scotland, helping him to become also James I of England. King James sought to reward Sir Archibald. Prime, unclaimed land being unavailable in Scotland, and titles without land empty, King James offered a royal patent for extensive lands in Ireland. Sir Archibald was given a considerable part of the county Armagh in Ulster, with the title Earl of Gosford. Today, his Acheson descendant sits in the House of Lords in Westminster holding that title. That Acheson lineage is uncertain in its connection with our family. My great-grandfather, Alexander Acheson, a non-commissioned officer in the Royal Artillery, fought with the Heavy Brigade at Balaclava in the Crimean War, but his records and family memorabilia did not survive his transfers in military life, or at least did not devolve to us, and we have only surmise as to his place and date of birth and his ancestral connections.

Family oral history has it that this same Alexander was from Armagh, that his first wife, my grandfather's mother (Mary Campion), died prematurely, and that a second wife did not have a good relationship with her young stepson, Edward Campion Acheson, my grandfather (born in 1857 at Aldershot, England). In any event, Edward went to Canada at university age to live with an uncle and study at Queen's College, Toronto. He became a student for the ministry at Wycliffe Theological Seminary there and enlisted in the Army upon the outbreak of the Riel Rebellion of 1883 in the Northwest Provinces.* His unit, the Queen's Own Rifles, was ambushed at Cut Knife Creek, and Edward emerged a national hero in circum-

*Louis Riel, a brilliant and controversial figure in Canadian history, organized an uprising of Indians and "Metis" in western Canada. He was executed in 1885 after conviction for treason.

Edward Campion Acheson at the time of the Northwest Rebellion of 1883 in
Canada.

Edward Campion Acheson as
a seminarian in Toronto, circa
1886 . . .

. . . and as a clergyman in New
York City, circa 1889.

stances best described in Mulvaney's *History of the Northwest Rebellion:*

> One incident of the fight cannot be left unrecorded. Private Acheson, of the Queen's Own, ran out from cover at the time the withdrawal was being made, to recover the body of Private Dodds, of the Battleford Rifles. Private Lloyd, of the Queen's Own, was near him at the time, and Acheson asked him to cover him while he went out. Lloyd did so, and went out to assist Acheson, who had shouldered the dead man. When they were returning Lloyd fell, shot in the back. He was in a stooping position when struck and the bullet, entering the centre of the back, penetrated up to the shoulder, under the blade. When Acheson had deposited the body under cover he at once returned to bring in Lloyd. Colour-Sergeant McKell, of the Queen's Own, went out to assist him, and between them they got Lloyd safely away from the enemy. It was a remarkable exhibition of heroism. The enemy were at moderately close range, and firing incessantly.*

Returning as a celebrated hero to Toronto, Edward met Eleanor Gooderham, the next to youngest of eleven children of George Gooderham, a very prominent and successful industrialist and banker of Toronto. Edward completed his divinity studies, was duly ordained, and he and Eleanor were married. He was called to his first church post as curate of a church in New York City. His next post was rector of the Church of the Holy Trinity in Middletown, Connecticut, where Eleanor and Edward settled in a roomy and handsome house on Washington Street, a gift of her father. There three children were raised, of whom Dad was the oldest and the first American citizen in the Acheson family.

Bishop Acheson (as my grandfather was at the time I knew him) was a handsome man and a vivid personality. He never

*C. P. Mulvaney, *The History of the Northwest Rebellion of 1883* (Toronto: A. H. Hovey & Co., 1885), pp. 169–71.

The Acheson residence in Middletown, Connecticut.

lost a noticeable British accent. He had a talent for entertaining young children. When we visited there in the late 1920s and early 1930s, a favorite breakfast dish of my grandparents was soft-boiled eggs. These were brought to the breakfast table, still in the unbroken shell, in a large oval china pot, of which the lid was sculpted as a sitting hen. Bishop Acheson, for the children's benefit, feigned puzzlement as to how to extract the eggs from beneath the watchful hen. Slowly he lifted the lid and cautiously slipped a hand beneath the hen. He then began an admonitory low clucking sound, perfectly authentic in pitch and verisimilitude. As his hand emerged holding an egg, the

Dean Gooderham Acheson
at age three.

clucking became alarmed, louder, and finally raucous. When the last egg was retrieved, everyone at the table was in hysterics.

From his military adventures in the Canadian West, my

Dean, Edward, and Margaret Acheson, circa 1896–97.

grandfather formed a fondness for a western tradition—throwing his hat through the door before entering a room in unfamiliar territory. When he visited us in Washington, where he attended occasional conferences of Episcopal bishops, he liked

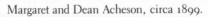

Margaret and Dean Acheson, circa 1899.

to look in on me in my third-floor room, where I labored over my homework before dinner. A light step on the creaky stair up to my aerie, a dramatic pause outside my door, then a black Homburg sailed through my door and landed on the floor, followed by a trim, erect figure below a handsome, smiling face. "Hello, David. Doing your sums, I see."

Bishop Acheson's vivid personality, a product of what Dad sometimes called a "wild Ulster streak," found reflections in all three of his children—Dean, Margaret, and Edward. All were more colorful than life, determinedly individual, almost ashamed of conformity. For Dad, it was a happy chance that he could serve in government at a time when individuality was respected and not regarded askance by conventional people and by the press as something *outré*.

Eleanor Gooderham Acheson as a young woman, camping in Canada.

On the opposite page: Edward Jr., Dean, Edward Campion Acheson, and Bob, circa 1910.

My grandmother ("Nan" to her grandchildren) sometimes told of Dad's estrangement from his father over an argument at the time Dad was a student at Yale. It might have been over the 1912 election campaign—Dad was an admirer of Theodore Roosevelt, his father of Taft. Whatever the argument, the term "fool" was injudiciously used by Dad, as in "only a fool could think that." Dad was exiled from the house forthwith, legend has it, for a year. This required Dad to spend vacations with his friends in San Francisco, New Orleans, and the Harriman residence on the Hudson, and opened up for him an early cosmopolitan view of the United States.

It was always hard for me to see my kindly and amusing grandfather in such an unforgiving role. The provocation must have been very great. In his youth, Dad had been mischievous and lighthearted, with a pronounced smart-aleck streak, and perhaps the erstwhile soldier was pushed too far. Earlier, at Groton School, Dad was judged by the Rector, Endicott Peabody, to be nonconformist and rebellious past all enduring, and Peabody summoned my grandmother to Groton to break the bad news that Dean had to go. In her firm but civil way, Nan proved tougher than Peabody. Nan's version of the celebrated conversation went like this:

PEABODY: *"Mrs. Acheson, I think it is clear that we will never be able to make a Groton boy out of Dean, and he would do well to go to another school."*

NAN: *"Dr. Peabody, I didn't send Dean here to have you make a 'Groton boy' out of him. I sent him here to be educated. Now, why do you feel you can't educate him?"*

PEABODY: *"Oh, we can educate him."*

NAN: *"Then I suggest you do it. I will leave him here as long as I think you can succeed, though you give me considerable doubt."*

PEABODY: *"Very well, then."*

Bishop Acheson, Nan, and Endicott Peabody were the Old World, and they lent to Dad's upbringing a distinctly nineteenth-century flavor. So also did his three senior law partners, J. Harry Covington, Edward B. Burling, and George Rublee.

Of Messrs. Covington and Rublee I had a slender acquaintance, derived from infrequent greetings at my parents' house, lasting into my teens. Mr. Burling I knew well, almost to the eve of my middle age. Judge Covington I recall as a handsome, good-natured, extroversive man of the world, a raconteur, with a mildly southern accent and a courtly, but informal, manner. He had been appointed to the appeals bench in the District of Columbia by President Wilson, and had left it to commence law practice in Washington with Mr. Burling immediately after World War I. The latter was a lawyer of renowned brilliance who had practiced in Chicago, come to Washington with the War Shipping Board in 1917, and then became Judge Covington's partner. He was tall and slim, with a crooked eye, a nineteenth-century way of combing his hair forward, and a quizzical, sardonic manner. He enjoyed playing the role of cynic, but had a deep capacity for generosity and friendship. I was lucky to have enjoyed his company and that friendship over many years. He affected Dad's life profoundly.

George Rublee was a very tall, grave, quiet man, whose face constantly wore an expression of great sadness, rather like a bloodhound. He was well connected in New York financial and

Dean Acheson (*front, center*) and Edward Campion Acheson (*front, right*) camping [note neckties], circa 1908.

Bishop Acheson and Eleanor Gooderham Acheson (Nan), circa 1927–28.

social circles, and through friends there was involved at one time as an investor in film productions in Mexico. He had a spirited wife, so that as a couple they marked off both the upper and lower limits of demonstrativeness. Mr. Rublee was the oldest living graduate of Groton School, and also its first graduate, comprising by himself the Class of 1886, a one-man class. He and Dad were close friends, and Mr. Rublee was kind enough to accompany Dad and me when we made our inspection trip to Groton in 1935, the year of my matriculation.

When Dad was law secretary to Justice Brandeis in 1919, the Justice invited him to lunch in chambers with a friend of the Justice, Edward B. Burling. "Mr. Burling plans to open a law office here in Washington shortly," said the Justice. Dad correctly thought of Washington practice at that time as a local practice of property, banking, and retail commerce matters. "What work will you do?" Dad asked of the guest. "Well," said Mr. Burling, "I have a notion that during this recent war government has formed the habit of regulating industry and will find that habit hard to break in peacetime." Truer words were never spoken, and Mr. Burling's fledgling partnership seized the leading edge of the new administrative law practice.

Years later, Mr. Burling wrote the most succinct account on record of the serendipity of the coming together of Covington, Burling, and Rublee:

. . . Rublee recommended me for a job in the newly formed Shipping Board. That is what brought me to Washington in August 1917.

I assumed that that would be a temporary war-time employment. But I never went back to Chicago. . . .

I was greatly indebted to George Rublee. I now had a chance to do him a good turn. In a short time, at my suggestion, he was made the

En route to Norway in 1922 to prepare their case for Norway in the Permanent Court of Arbitration at The Hague. *Left to right:* Edward B. Burling, Dean Acheson, George Rublee, and Walter L. Fisher.

third member of the firm, and it became Covington, Burling & Rublee.

George Rublee's contribution to the firm was quite as important as any contribution made by me and nearly as important as any made by Judge Covington. . . .

Judge Covington was a duck hunter. George told members of J. P. Morgan & Company of Judge Covington and his duck blinds on the Chesapeake Bay.

As a result, Morgan partners spent weekends shooting ducks with Judge Covington.

The Judge made a great hit with them. He had a long list of Southern anecdotes.

So, when the wreckage caused by the War had to be settled, these New York lawyers and businessmen turned to Covington for help, much of it by way of Rublee.

This, initiated by Rublee, is what gave the firm its first great success.

Without Covington, there would have been no ducks, no Southern anecdotes, and no New York connection. Without Rublee those New York financiers would never have heard of Covington—much less of me.*

This is not mere digression into the personalities of Dad's senior law partners. They were the chief conduit by which the values of originality, individuality, and service were encouraged in the young lawyer. No one has more succinctly stated this influence than Dad himself, speaking about Mr. Burling on the occasion of the celebration of Mr. Burling's second marriage (at ninety-three!):

The young men Mr. Burling took into his office were not employees; they became wards to whose education, in the broadest sense, he devoted his high intelligence and great capacity for human relationship. He wanted them to be tough and competent in their profession;

*The quotations are taken from a 1965 speech by Mr. Burling to the partners of Covington & Burling. It is reprinted in *Reflections: Writings by Edward Burnham Burling and Tributes by his Friends* (1966).

but, more than that, he taught them to deal with their lives adventur-
ously and vigorously, not to coddle themselves within the safe con-
fines of conventional success. Preeminently, he wanted them to free
their minds for thought, thought ranging far beyond the platitudes of
the usual Washington talk. Speculation was his method and Socrates
was his model. No thesis was, or is, too startling for him to espouse
and, espousing, to shake successive generations out of enticing com-
placency.*

This description was, of course, not merely an affectionate trib-
ute to Mr. Burling but a pithy statement of Dad's own intellectual values, saying as much about him as his venerable partner.

That Dad's law practice was not without its lighter side is
evidenced by a note he received in 1936 from Harry L. Hopkins, then WPA Administrator and later President Roosevelt's
most trusted staff adviser. The note concerned a case in which
Dad represented electric power utilities which sought to enjoin
and prevent the construction of public power projects, the latter being pushed by Hopkins:

Dean Acheson
Counselor-at-Law

Dear Sir:
The idea of your claiming that a power project, approved three years
ago and still unbuilt, has not provided employment is a clear evidence
of prejudice on your part. A good Democratic architect, six detectives
and a publicity man have been paid out of this project for years. Their
jobs may last forever if you can only keep this in the courts long
enough. And this case of Tugwell's—are you in on that? Books will be
written about it—this will provide employment. I can make out a
good case to prove that there will be more employment if the projects
are never built.

H.L.H.†

*From Dean Acheson's typed notes.
†This note was written in longhand on the back of the menu of the Washing-

There are not many profiles extant of Dad as a lawyer, and only one that conveys a considered peer opinion. That one was delivered by the Honorable Gerhard A. Gesell, U.S. District Judge (in the District of Columbia), in memorial proceedings in his court shortly after Dad's death in October 1971. Judge Gesell said:

. . . He was a well-rounded lawyer. His practice was not only an office practice but it was a courtroom practice that involved trial work, appellate work and agency work both in the national arena and internationally.

He had an extraordinary facility of picking up his professional undertakings after periods of public service with ease. He had a flair for the written and spoken word. He was a master of the beauty and subtlety of language and he turned that to an extraordinarily high performance in the briefs he wrote and in the written and oral advice that he gave.

He was precise, careful, discriminating and persuasive; and was known for the high standard of his work. A stern critic of younger lawyers, he also could not be easily manipulated by a client. While I do not intend to breach any confidences, he not always gave opinions that clients wanted. When the Treasury was his client, he refused to give an opinion, which he knew would lead to his departure from Government service. . . .

He could quickly see the realities of an issue. He worked with intense energy; he was highly productive; he didn't suffer fools gladly; and perhaps his often severity in public appearances as a lawyer is the reason that not everyone recognized the extraordinary charm, wit and humor of the man.

He was widely read, full of anecdotes when talking with his intimates and had the grace and good fortune to be one of those rare people who could laugh at himself.

---

ton Hotel dining room where Hopkins and Acheson presumably were at lunch, though probably not together.

Dean Acheson as an artilleryman home from Tobyhanna, with his mother, 1915.

Pater Familias

D AD WAS ALWAYS a strong family man, that is to say, he cared for his family, held a deep affection for its members, and made numerous sacrifices for their collective and individual welfares. He was brought up that way. There was a close bond between Dad and his mother, née Eleanor Gooderham, of Toronto. She was one of eleven children and grew up in a close-knit family in which children and parents sailed, camped, shot, fished, and followed cultural pursuits together. She was affectionate and humorous, and doubtless sought to bring to her own family the values that she knew before her marriage. Nan, as she was called, tended to indulge her children, and they adored her uncritically. In *Morning and Noon,* Dad wrote of his first job on a railway construction crew in Canada in the summer of 1911 and how he spent his summer's earnings on a present for his mother, a brooch which she wore until her death.

Dad's father, Bishop Acheson, was a kindly man, fond of his children but conditioned in that respect by his tour of combat duty in the Queen's Own Rifles in 1883–84. Affection and a strong sense of discipline were never far separated in his parental relations.

Dad brought to parenting values similar to those he had experienced as a child. Family group activity should be frequent, instructive, outdoors, vigorous, and (if possible), fun. He was fortunate to have married (in 1917) a lady who shared many of his recreational interests, Alice Caroline Stanley, of Detroit, Michigan. They met through the intercession of

Margaret, Edward Jr., and Dean Acheson (the latter very likely in church dress), circa 1916.

Margaret Acheson, Dad's sister, who befriended Alice Stanley at Wellesley College. Attraction of opposites might have had something to do with their friendship. Alice Stanley was a classic brunette beauty, artistic, reserved, raised in a midwest family of strong independence and a high regard for education. Margaret Acheson, or Margot, was a flamboyant, glamorous, beautiful redhead who regarded social conventions as testing obstacles put in the way of talented people to be overcome. Alice and Margot were lifetime friends through Margot's marriage, divorce, remarriage, childrearing, illnesses, until Margot's death in 1959.

Alice Stanley, by her own account, was the first student in Wellesley College's history to be married and allowed to graduate. What role Dad actually played in what must have been a delicate negotiation is not recorded, but it may have been less than he liked to claim. His version was simply that he won his first case on oral argument while he was still at law school. They were married in May of 1917.

So far as children can judge these things, the relations between my parents were affectionate and companionable until the day of Dad's death. Such frictions as arose seem, in retrospect, to have been the occasional static electricity generated by two strong characters. Mother was made of flinty material, capable of telling Winston Churchill (as a painter) that his palette was "too bright," capable of telling Henry Kissinger (as National Security Adviser) that the Acheson dinner hour was at hand and he must terminate his meeting with Dad and go. Mother had profoundly ingrained attitudes that no subsequent experience would change: about food—it should be plain and not pretentious; about church—it should be plain and not pretentious; about people—they should be plain and not pretentious. There was more than a hint of Michigan Calvinism here. Dad liked more of the baroque in life—in food, church services, and people. But Mother had much in common with Dad: reading, outdoor recreation, love of travel, gardening and working around their farm.

Between Mother and Dad there appeared to be a clear division of labor. Mother hired and fired the children's nurses and the domestic help. Mother planned the meals and ordered the food. Dad decided upon the children's schools, and carried out selections and purchases of cars. Together, Mother and Dad effected several successful plans for improvement and enlargement of the Georgetown house and the buildings at the farm. Their partnership was durable because it was firmly based on commonly held major premises by which both lived.

As the children grew, intra-family relations, while always affectionate, grew more complex. Jane and I were raised when spanking was a familiar parental tool carrying pediatric approbation. In our house it was not neglected. Each of us had a strong streak of rebelliousness, which invited spanking, and a robust sense of personal dignity, which made us resent the experience more than we profited by it. Mary seemingly learned from our unedifying examples and her rearing followed a more tranquil course. But by and large we were a close family; we had fun together and enjoyed each other's company. All of us were shipped away to boarding school in our early teens, in my case at least partly because it was hoped that I would benefit from a "taut ship," but it did not appear to weaken our family bonds.

Early in her life Mother took up painting and early in her

Jane Acheson and the author, circa 1924.

marriage she became a professional painter. She attended the
first painting class at the Corcoran Gallery in Washington.
Like her mother—a vivid and accomplished watercolorist—
Mother worked mainly in watercolors in her early professional
years. She soon branched out into oil, painting in both media
landscapes, scenes of people and animals, street scenes and
buildings. Still later, she expanded to work in collage and "drib-
ble." Her work was a true reflection of the soul behind it—of
strong lines and colors, conveying a vivid and distinctive per-
ception of the subject.

Dad strongly encouraged Mother's work, liked the product, and faithfully attended her numerous exhibitions. Over the years his various office locations were liberally decorated with Mother's work, as were their children's rooms, college lodgings and, in later years, their homes.

Though Dad could be an intimidating disciplinarian, it was only when his children disappointed him or breached his insistence upon civility and duty. He was not a martinet over little things. Generally, he tried to communicate a positive message of correction, conveying the domestic policy that was transgressed, the rationale behind it, the harm done by the transgression, and the change of conduct that would serve domestic policy. Sometimes his Celtic temperament was not quite equal to the burden of reasoned correction and there was a flair of anger that left feelings hurt and personal dignity offended. He was probably more sorely tried—and more frequently—than we children realized, particularly when we three hit our teens in the 1930s, the time of automobile mishaps and gauche encounters with the opposite sex.

It was not until we three went away to school that we became parties to Dad's habit of correspondence, much of it in longhand, all of it thoughtful and mind-expanding. Then Dad wrote frequently, about the threatening developments in the Far East and in Europe, about events in Washington (which Dad always regarded in a lighthearted vein), about our respective academic performances, about home life and events befalling the house, dogs, horses, etc. I became aware at this time (mid-1930s) that Dad was an articulate and perceptive writer and observer, even an elegant stylist. To what extent he exceeded the norm in these respects, I was not to appreciate until

I had a much wider acquaintance with the published diaries and correspondence of public men. A few examples of Dad's letters will convey the genre:

. . . Alice and I went up to New York on Thursday, where I went to a class dinner and she went to the theater. We stayed with the Douglases. We then went on to New Haven and had a very pleasant time there. I spoke to the law students on Friday evening, and later went back to another law student meeting, where Harold Laski was carrying on a competition in being bright with some of the more vocal young men. He patronized Mr. Thatcher, Mr. Taft and me, which gave him a great deal of pleasure and did us no visible harm.*

. . . On Saturday evening Charlie Seymour had a dinner for the Corporation and reception at his new house. The house, which was left to the University, has been remodeled at tremendous expense to it and is much too grand. However, some people seem to believe that a college president should live like a Sultan of Bagdad. We certainly have provided such a background. The evening which started out as a great success ended in a minor disaster. The Seymours gave us a beautiful dinner, one item of which was the lobster. This destroyed the President, although the rest of us survived. In the midst of the reception at the School of Fine Arts, when he was shaking hands with several thousand people, he became the most beautiful green color and had to be taken home and put to bed.

My love, as ever,†

When my sister, Mary Acheson Bundy, was ill at Saranac Lake with tuberculosis in the mid-1940s, Dad wrote her every evening, keeping her tuned in to the life of the house and the broader life of Washington, a long series of letters of sharp, irreverent, pithy observations, quite in the vein of private cocktail-hour gossip.

*Letter to David C. Acheson, April 12, 1937, *Among Friends*, p. 31.
†Letter to David C. Acheson, Dec. 13, 1937, *Among Friends*, p. 34.

Dad liked to write. Invariably, whether letters, briefs, articles or books, he wrote in longhand, all but letters on a legal size, yellow ruled pad. He wrote in a script bearing the mark of an Edwardian era education, an idiosyncratic hand of sharp angles and Greek E's. He had a native instinct for elegant and distinctive syntax and for the arresting figure of speech. His children looked forward to his letters for their tart humor and their way of peeling the bark from the subject.

When spouses of his children came into the picture, Dad modulated his relations with them quite precisely. They stood midway between children and friends, clearly distinguishable from children and further away from parental authority and intimacy, but more amenable to confidences and candor than mere friends. None of his children-in-law would let him cross that delicate line. An occasional skirmish reminded Dad that he was not dealing with puppets, that affection was not fealty.

While, in retrospect, we seemed to live well in the 1920s and 1930s, Dad's books were never far into the black. Dad's maternal grandfather, a merchant and banker in Toronto, was a very rich man, but he had eleven children; subdivision upon his death and conservatively invested trust funds for my grandmother left her comfortably off, but not really affluent. Mother and Dad began their marriage with no capital and wholly dependent, first upon the salary of a young naval officer, then of a law secretary of a Supreme Court Justice, then of a young associate in a fledgling Washington law firm. It was not until Dad became a partner in 1926 that he began earning anything substantial. His period of full-time practice only ran from then until early 1941, when he went into the State Department at a salary (I think) of $8,000 a year. Dad's peak year as a lawyer was

Christmas in Middletown, Connecticut, 1930. *From left, rear:* Eleanor Gooderham Acheson (Nan), Dean Acheson, Margaret Acheson Ryder Platt, Alice Acheson, Gardiner Platt, Elizabeth Acheson, and Bishop Acheson. *From left, front:* Eleanor Ryder, Mary Acheson, Jane Acheson, the author, and Edward Acheson, Jr. (Ted).

probably 1940, when I recall him telling me he earned a bit more than $80,000, a lot less than the incomes earned at the New York firms. Except for a year and a half back at Covington & Burling in 1947–48, Dad was on government salary from 1941 through 1952, at ages forty-eight to sixty, the peak years for most lawyers.

When Dad returned to his firm in 1953, matters were very different from the ways things are today. Lawyers then did not earn the large incomes of today. More importantly, the retiring Secretary of State was not the magnet to client business that many might suppose. The Truman administration was anathema to the largely Republican worlds of industry and finance, the chief sources of major legal business. Dad went back to his firm in 1953 essentially as a pensioner and stared at the wall for a time. He managed to get some episodic legal business in the 1950s and 1960s, even a few important cases, but never reacquired his professional standing of the prewar years. It was both boredom and financial motivation that led Dad to take up writing articles and books, and by the late 1950s he had become a full-time writer.

During the 1930s and 1940s, one must recall, the life that Mother and Dad led was not costly to maintain. Boarding school charges ran in the $2,000 to $3,000 per annum range, one fortieth of a prosperous lawyer's income. Horses, feed, even land, were cheap. A really good car could be had for $1,500 or 2 percent of an income of $80,000, as opposed to $30,000, or 10 percent of an income of $300,000, today. While Mother and Dad were always conscious of the limits of their means, in my youth a dollar seemed to buy a lot. The menu of the Hotel Washington in 1936 (on which Harry Hopkins addressed his note to Dad) shows prices of $1.00 for the table d'hôte luncheon, 35 cents for cherrystone clams, 90 cents for sautéed soft shell crabs, 70 cents for lamb chop with bacon. Dad bought his 120-acre farm 18 miles from Washington in 1924 (actually a period of post–World War I inflation) for $100 an acre. So, in those days a farm, horses, a tennis court, private schools, a swimming pool did not carry anything like the implications of affluence that they might today.

The Strenuous Life
at Harewood Farm

WHEN MY SISTERS and I were very young (single-digit ages), Mother and Dad bought a small farm in Maryland about eighteen miles north of Washington and twenty-eight miles north of our city house, probably in 1924. It was an old farm, about 120 acres of land, situated a mile southwest of Route 29, which was the back road to Ellicott City and Baltimore from Washington. The date, 1792, was stamped on a brick in the breast of the fireplace in the dining room. Dad bought the farm from one Edward Stabler, whose family had owned it for quite a few generations. A printing and engraving shop had been operated by the Stablers in a large detached building, where the old drive-wheels still hung from the ceiling. There some official seals for federal cabinet departments had been struck about the time of Andrew Jackson, of which we later acquired trial drawings. Dad converted the engraving shop to a guest house, installed running water and a match-lit kerosene water heater, so that guests had privacy and a fair degree of comfort, though the thirty-yard stretch from house to guest house was patrolled by skunks at night and bees by day.

About half a mile north of the farmhouse was the village of Sandy Spring, consisting of a bank, an insurance firm, a general store, post office, gas station, and a few houses. A mile west of there lay the Montgomery County Hospital. Sandy Spring had been settled by Quakers not long after the Toleration Acts had become law in Lord Baltimore's colony. Names familiar in other Quaker settlements in the eastern United States were familiar in Sandy Spring—Hallowell, Thomas, Farquhar. A few hundred yards south of the center of the village was the Quaker Meeting House, a building of old red brick and of

Dean Acheson in the guest house of Harewood Farm. The drive wheels of the nineteenth century print shop are overhead. PHOTO: © JILL KREMENTZ

much charm and dignity. It lay right on the road between our farm and the village. The Meeting had built a semicircular by-pass to carry traffic away from the Meeting House during meeting hours on Sunday, an accommodation scrupulously observed by drivers and horseback riders.

Nothing much hurried in Sandy Spring, except the volunteer fire department. Civility and calm were almost tangible. Courtesy begat courtesy. Elderly ladies wore velvet chokers and wide-brimmed straw hats. Sometimes a lorgnette dangled from a lady's neck on a thin gold chain. Often an automobile (it was the age of the Model T Ford; the Model A came along at the end of the 1920s) sported a glass vase on the window post with a rosebud in it.

In the early years at the farm, no one whom I can remember in the Sandy Spring community, beside my father, lived and worked in Washington.* It was not a "bedroom" community, but a real community. Its sole bank had a reputation for the highest competence and integrity, as did its adjacent insurance firm. The bank never broke stride during the Great Depression.

The farmhouse at Harewood Farm, for such was our farm's name, had no heat until the 1940s. This had profound consequences. The house could only be occupied in warm weather, which, with school schedules, really meant summer. In the cold weather we often made day trips from Washington to clear woods and cut brush. Dad had strong views on clearing woods. He liked trees to stand in a "deer park," as he put it, with no

---

*Harold Ickes, best known as President Roosevelt's Secretary of the Interior, bought a farm at Olney, a couple of miles away, in the mid-1930s.

Harewood Farm: Main house from the north.

Burning brush: Alice and Dean Acheson; and Dudley Brown (*right*), Jane Acheson's husband.

underbrush to snag the royal feet. On Saturday or Sunday, school homework permitting, we bundled off to the farm for a picnic lunch outdoors and a day in the woods. Pathways through the woods were widened for horseback riding, and saplings which threatened the light and space of an established tree were doomed.

These expeditions were well equipped. Laura, the Washington cook, provided tomato, turkey and roast beef sandwiches, and a thermos of hot soup, usually the universal favorite, Philadelphia pepper pot. To sustain flagging juvenile morale on the fifty-minute drive from Georgetown to Sandy Spring, there was a box of salt crackers and tins of deviled ham, for which Dad taught us a barely controlled addiction. Dad was a purposive, but not harsh, taskmaster. We were to work until 1:00 P.M., then build an outdoor brush fire and have our picnic lunch, then work until failing light. If the cold was intense, a small silver flask emerged from the picnic hamper and a few drops of a mysterious liquid were poured into each cup of soup. This never failed to buoy mind and body, like "the distant triumph song" in the hymn *For All the Saints*, which made hearts brave again, and arms strong.

Dad's summer job on the Canadian railroad crew had taught him well in the matter of tools.* A small timber saw, an ax, and a couple of brush hooks were standard equipment. The brush hook was Dad's favorite tool. It was (and is) a cutting tool about the weight of an ax, with a similar handle. The blade, however, is about twelve inches long and curved inward toward

---

*See the Appendix for the text of a letter from Dad to Endicott Peabody, Rector of Groton School, describing this experience.

the single cutting edge, to about a 45-degree angle. This shape gives the blade its distinctive hook appearance, rather resembling weapons carried by the *sans-culottes*, rural revolutionaries depicted in paintings of the French Revolution. For us, the brush hook was a lethal weapon, easily dispatching a one- or two-inch sapling, sharp as a knife, heavy as an ax. One swung it at ground level, pulling back a bit at the end of the stroke so the hook tip would sever any small stuff that got in the way. Dad could eliminate a quarter acre of brush, or more, in a couple of hours. The standard drill was to burn the brush as one worked, so the fire was never very big or dangerous. One cut and raked outward from the selected fire site, so there was an ever-widening area of bare earth between the fire and anything else of a combustible nature.

Dad organized the work in a simple way, wholly unaware of any latent feminist issue. He and I handled the brush hook and ax, and the infrequent sawing tasks. The women raked the cuttings to the brush pile and tended the fire, watching for any fingers of flame that might reach out to leaves or any possible firepath into uncleared territory.

One day of particular memory was unseasonably warm. Dad shed his tweed overcoat to work and pretty soon was cutting brush many yards away from the brush fire, which was not being diligently watched. At the lunch break Dad looked for his coat to put it on again. "Alice," he called to Mother, "where's my coat?" "Probably just where you left it," came the crisp reply. Sure enough, just where he left it there were three buttons on a fire-blackened patch of ground. The coat had gone up in smoke.

Dad liked order, and order required preparation. When

horseback riding became a frequent family activity, it was not enough to clear overgrown riding paths through the woods. It also was necessary to build "chicken coop" jumps over wire fences, since horses cannot see the wire to jump. This was a simpler matter than it might seem. Again, the railroad section gang had taught well. We selected a crossing point on a fence, where there was clear ground on both sides. Then we built two simple three-piece "A-frames" of 2″ by 4″ lumber. The A was at 90 degrees to the line of the fence, so the two sides of the triangle were on opposite sides of the fence, joining the bottom side at ground level. We usually cheated a bit and depressed the wire as we nailed up the A-frames, so that the top of the jump would be a few inches lower than the prevailing height of the fence. Then we nailed 1″ by 6″ planks to the A-frames so that both frames were joined by the planks on both sides of the fence. The result was a sort of wooden tent, or "chicken coop," covering a six-foot section of fence. It was not strictly legal to do this where the fence separated Acheson property from a neighbor's, but Dad always claimed to have some sort of understanding with the neighbor on whatever border of the farm we might be working. I think he really believed this.

At the time, I was struck by Dad's self-confidence in such field construction work, and by the purpose and dispatch of execution. It was a teaching experience, and taught both the skill and the affection for such work which have never left me and which my sons share.

Chicken-cooping fences was work which generally proceeded away from the presence of the family women. In these circumstances Dad's language sometimes yielded to a momentary frustration, and it became clear that not all of his English came from Groton and Yale. Not infrequently we drove to the fence site and had forgotten the measuring tape or the level or the nails. Not infrequently Dad hit his finger with the hammer or snagged his clothes on barbed wire. Then some choice expletives poured forth—not simple, vulgar obscenities at all, but rich, imaginative cursing, sometimes using terms I had never heard before and have not heard since. The Lord's name was not merely taken in vain, but summoned to work ruin in ingenious ways on inanimate objects that failed to behave as Dad thought they should. What a shame that there is no oral history of the Canadian Pacific Railroad section gang or of the Yale Battery at Tobyhanna where these rich oaths were taught!

When these occasions had passed, Dad often cautioned me, somewhat sheepishly, that he had yielded to an irresistible impulse, that I was not to take this lapse as an acceptable model, and, indeed, I would get into a lot of trouble if I had a similar lapse. Alas, these disclaimers were never half so convincing as the original lapse; I was never able to form a code of conduct on the basis of "do as I say, not as I do." And I did narrowly avoid serious trouble at school for following the example.

A background digression about Tobyhanna, Pennsylvania, is pertinent here. In the summer of 1915, the looming national security threat was the likelihood of war with Mexico. The Yale Battery, a field artillery training unit, went to Tobyhanna for training exercises. It was hilly, rocky country, with undependable water resources. Almost immediately the caisson horses began to fall sick. Some died. These had to be buried in what was essentially granite with a shallow covering of soil. So backbreaking was the labor that every man became a tender nurse for the sick horses. As more horses fell ill, all other duties were suspended and every man bent all effort to save the sick horses. One night a surprise inspection of the camp was made by the great soldier-politician of the time, General Leonard Wood. Near midnight, Private Acheson was on guard duty at the stable. Flashlights and footsteps approached, and he challenged the intruders, "Who goes there?" The reply came back, "The commanding general of the Eastern Department." "Advance

Palladio at Harewood Farm.

and be recognized," said the shaken sentry. It was, indeed, General Wood, who then interrogated the sentry: "Private, what are your duties here?" "Guarding the horses, sir." "Now Private, what would you do if one of these horses were to get sick?" Dad was astounded at the ignorance of the question. "Christ, General, they're *all* sick!" He was roundly reprimanded for his unmilitary demeanor, but at least had put the facts of life on the table.

Around 1930, Mother and Dad started their practice of living at the farm for the summer, once the school year was over. Dad drove in every day to his law practice at Covington, Burling & Rublee where, a few years before, he had become a partner. Beside clothing, some items of furniture were moved seasonally from, and back to, the Georgetown house. Moving day was a big deal. An open truck was hired and in it went suitcases, trunks, and a few beds, bureaus, and chairs. The big event of the early summer for us children was to ride in the open truck to the country—a bumpy and wind-blown experience. Dad usually succeeded in absenting himself from the actual moving operation and came home to the farm at the end of the day when everything and everybody had settled nicely into place.

Dad loved the farm, the cool evenings, cocktails on the lawn, the physically demanding weekends of riding, building chicken coop jumps over fences, working on the gravel road and drainage ditches, the drive through the countryside to and from Washington, the nineteenth-century civility of the Sandy Spring community. He liked waking to the sound of birds and the mooing of cows in his and the neighbor's fields. He liked being a rural squire with responsibility for a tenant farmer and for farm animals. He kept some Hereford cattle and four or five horses, became friendly with the admirable veterinarian, Dr. Ladson, and took time and care for the health of his livestock. The union of man and nature really meant much to him, something he never experienced in the city.

Dr. Ladson was a memorable and exemplary man and veterinarian. Both expert and gentle in his handling of animals, he inspired immediate confidence in beast and owner. He could put medicine capsules down a horse's throat when no one else could even coax the horse to stand still. To watch him soothe a horse, administer novocaine, and cut away and bandage skin torn by barbed wire was, to me, close to a religious experience. Everyone admired Dr. Ladson. His children became our friends and were much like him.

Before my parents built a swimming pool—about 1937–38—the chief swimming resource was the Patuxent River, a stream perhaps thirty to forty yards wide which wound through Howard County a few miles east of Sandy Spring. Dad believed rivers were for swimming, so off we went, *en famille,* to swim in the murky water of the Patuxent. It was difficult swimming for children—from place to place a muddy or rocky bottom, hard to stand, harder still to see to the bottom. Our lobbying for a swimming pool had its origin in the muddy banks and bottom of the Patuxent. That river looked to me like the illustrations of the great, gray-green, greasy Limpopo River in Kipling's story, *How the Elephant Got Its Trunk.* The elephant got its trunk in a tug-of-war for its nose, with a crocodile. The trees overhanging the Patuxent were right out of the Limpopo illustrations ("all set about with fever trees") and I was certain that the crocodile's cousin was right here in the Patuxent. Dad was vastly amused by my fears, but in the end an anxiety over typhoid fever 'and polio ended our tests of character in the Patuxent.

Self-interest was at work. Dad liked to swim, but found the Patuxent messy and the typhoid-polio risks remote but finite. The Manor Club pool, near Norbeck about six miles away, was heavily chlorinated and turned our eyes red. The subject of a swimming pool entered our dining-room conversation more and more often, but for some years the ancient farmhouse, other old and decaying buildings, and the water pumps pre-empted the available funds. Then, a water dowser appeared one day and proceeded to search for water in a little dale at the edge of the woods by the field behind the house. No one needed a rat's hip bone or a willow wand to guess there might be water in that declivity, and sure enough, there it was, at about 70 feet and 60 gallons a minute. We had hit an underground stream, perhaps

> Where Alph, the sacred river, ran
> Through caverns measureless to man
> Down to a sunless sea.

The good news was that we had plenty of water for a pool. The bad news was that it was ice water, as near gelid as running water can be. But that was not fully understood until the pool was built and filled. Those who have swum on the Maine coast may have some idea of the paralyzing effect of that degree of cold. So clear was the water, only reflections could be seen in the pool. Dad called it "the two-Martini" pool: it took one to make you brave enough to go in, and you needed another to restart your heart when you got out. In later years, well after World War II, the pool was heated, but we went through many years of character building through pain.

Beginning in the prewar years, Archibald MacLeish sometimes came to visit at the farm. He was my father's closest friend from the Yale Class of 1915, where Archie had been a star varsity football player and captain of the water polo team, as well as premier scholar and head of the *Yale Literary Magazine*. Archie's great feat in the eyes of the Achesons was his underwater swim down the length of our pool and back, 120 feet, with a racing turn off the wall at the halfway point, all of this without coming up for breath. The ice water simply made the challenge interesting for Archie. He performed the same feat for me in his own pool in Conway, Massachusetts, in 1979 when he was eighty-six.

Dad, on the other hand, had no highly developed water

The ice-water swimming pool at Harewood Farm, circa 1950. *Foreground:* The author with Eleanor Dean Acheson. *Right background:* Dean Acheson.

skills. He had been an oarsman at Groton and Yale; his perspective was from above the water, not from beneath the surface. He did not dive, believing that immersion of the head induced baldness. He swam with his head fully out of the water, arms coming forward, body fully submerged. He entered the water from the shallow end, pushing off the shallow bottom into the deep water with a great frontal splash, rather like the launching of a ship, creating a small tsunami at the end of the pool. When he swam, he filled his cheeks with air which he blew out over the surface of the water, his mustache bristling with the facial motion. The effect was rather that of a large seal with prominent reddish eyebrows, both comic and alarming. Small children squealed with mixed delight and apprehension.

Dad and Uncle Ted introduced an elaborate entertainment to the swimming pool. At the shallow end was a concrete spillway, which let surface water run out of the pool when fresh water was pumped in at the bottom and forced the water level up. This kept the pool reasonably fresh. One could stop the spillway at the pool edge by putting a board down across the spillway in slots set in the concrete for that purpose. The spillway ran down a bank so the bottom was perhaps twenty feet or more below the top, and ended in a widened mouth several feet in width. The game was to stop the spillway with the board and, at the wide mouth below the bank, construct a small, crude village of mud and twigs. Then the board was removed and a catastrophic cataract washed down the spillway and swept the village away. Dad named this game "Johnstown," after the Pennsylvania town swept away in the collapse of a dam in 1889. Our villages became increasingly elaborate until we lost the will to destroy them and the game lost its point.

Firearms played a small but steady part in the life of the farm. Dad liked to shoot clay pigeons and a supply was always at hand. He wished to teach me to shoot, as his father had taught him. My first gun was a small single-shot .410-gauge shotgun made by L. C. Smith. It had no recoil to speak of and was an excellent training gun. Dad mounted a clay pigeon launcher trap on a 12" x 12" log. The standard drill was to carry the trap and its mounting to the field behind the guest house

The author takes a shot.

and launch the targets out across the field, away from the buildings. It took a lot of muscle to cock the launcher against the heavy spring, powerful enough to throw the clay disc, spinning like a Frisbee, seventy-five yards or more. When the gunner said "Pull," the trap operator pulled the lanyard that tripped the spring, and the clay pigeon took off like a quail. A hit often powdered the pigeon in a brief, black puff; most satisfying. One could elevate or depress the trap so that the disc could light out at nearly ground level or rise sharply into the air.

Both Dad and I became quite adept, and soon I graduated to a 20-gauge double-barreled shotgun.

At this time, Dad's mother lived in Middletown, Connecticut. She was widowed in 1934 and in the next few years visited occasionally at the farm. She was one of a large brood, men and women, of a great merchant leader of Toronto, and had been schooled by her father in all the ways of the Canadian woods: boats, camping, and firearms. By the mid-1930s she was around seventy years of age, a tall, slender, graceful woman of great dignity and presence and of keen mind and common sense. She wore two basic dresses, of which she had many copies: a black lace dress and a cream lace dress, both to ankle length, black for fall and winter, cream for spring and summer. I did not know it until the event I report here, but she was a crack shot, nearly a circus shot. She often sat at her desk in Middletown, doing her correspondence, with the window open facing the pine trees at the end of her garden, perhaps fifty yards from her window. Red squirrels had been raiding birds' nests in the trees. Nan more than once was seen by her maid to take a loaded .22 rifle from her desk, and—CRACK!—a red squirrel dropped from a tree.

On Nan's visit that I write of, Dad suggested that we shoot some clay pigeons after lunch. We set up the trap and offered Nan her choice of weapons: a single-shot .410 gauge (the bore a little thicker than a cigarette), my 20 gauge, or Dad's 12 gauge (with a heavy recoil). Nan chose the .410. "But Mother, you can't hit anything with a .410—the shot pattern is too small." "Never mind, dear, I like a light gun." We loaded the clay pigeon into the trap, aimed the trap low, and angled to the left, a difficult shot. Nan called "Pull" in a firm, clear voice, and off went the clay bird. About thirty feet out we saw a puff of black clay powder and heard the BAM! simultaneously. "That wasn't hard," was Nan's comment. Then we gave her a wide, rising shot to the right, and then a sharp rising shot at maximum elevation, and finally a "grounder," a quail going for close cover. All were dead birds, four for four.

The following September, I wrote a paper for school on the science and sport of clay pigeon shooting. In it I described our scoring system: for each hit, the gunner put the spent shell in his pocket. At the end of the match, one counted one's spent shells. I showed the completed paper to Dad. He had one comment: "Considering Mother's performance, you ought to say 'his or her pocket.' " I agreed. It seemed the least I could do.

Years later, during World War II, Dad recalled this extraordinary talent of his mother when he found himself in Atlantic City for an international conference about postwar relief. He wrote his mother: " . . . On the rare occasions when I get out of the Hotel—I have passed the shooting galleries or their successors which you and I used to frequent and where you used to so amaze the proprietors."[*]

Life at the farm in the 1930s was not uniformly recreational or pastoral for Dad. His weekends were often punctuated by the arrival of younger lawyers at the Covington firm to work with him on a brief, for whatever litigation then engaged his attention. Dad and his visitor regularly disappeared into the

*Letter to Eleanor Gooderham Acheson, Nov. 27, 1943, *Among Friends*, p. 43.

guest house for several hours of work, equipped with pencils and yellow pads, for such was the technology of brief writing at that time. If Dad's weekend had to be interrupted by legal work, he wanted to have control of the interruption. If he went into the office, he knew the day was shot.

Dad's professional practice in the prewar years was largely given to legal business in the courts and federal agencies in Washington that lawyers out of town referred to the Covington firm. Occasionally, the importunities of some of those out-of-town lawyers impinged painfully on Dad's peace and quiet. An egregious case involved a very distinguished partner of a prominent New York firm—we will call him Mr. K—with whom Dad had done considerable legal business. One Friday night, in the wee hours, Dad's sleep at the farm was shattered by the telephone. It was a distraught Mr. K. His daughter had driven to visit a friend in Washington, had run out of gas north of Washington, had been threatened by a man on the road, been rescued by the Montgomery County Police, and was even now at the police headquarters in Rockville. She was a willful and flighty girl who needed parental guidance and custody. Would Dad do a great favor: drive to Rockville and bring Miss K back to the farm for what remained of the night, reunite her with her car on the morrow, and see that she reached the family that was her destination? Dad would have preferred to wrestle an alligator, but saw that he could give none but an affirmative response. He dressed and drove over to Rockville, twenty-five minutes away.

Not surprisingly, Miss K's drama had quickly become known to all the police staff and to the police reporters who covered the crime beat. When Dad arrived at police headquarters, Miss K, totally unharmed, had completed her statement about her recent perils and was sitting on a desk, showing an interesting length of leg, having her picture shot from all sides by a bevy of photographers. Dad identified himself to the sergeant, signed an appearance—in effect, a receipt for Miss K—and told Miss K in no uncertain terms that she was to come with him at once, under orders from her father. But Miss K was enjoying herself. "Just one more shot, please, Miss K. Just one more," as the flash bulbs exploded. Dad had now progressed from impatience to irritation. He grabbed Miss K by the arm, yanked her off the desk, and pushed her out the door, his face set in an expression that boded bodily harm, as the flash bulbs exploded one more time. That face, fixed on Miss K's retreating back, appeared in the *Washington Evening Star* the next day over the caption: "New York Girl Eludes Attacker"! Such were the hazards of a referral practice.

Cavaliers

P ERHAPS I WAS SEVEN OR EIGHT YEARS OLD when Dad
was smitten by the equestrian passion. Like some of
his other enthusiasms for sport, this one developed
abruptly, like an autumn hurricane boiling out of a low pressure
area. But it did not come out of nowhere. Dad had learned to
be a competent, though far from expert, horseman from his
father's teaching and from training with the Yale Battery at the
field artillery camp at Tobyhanna, Pennsylvania. By the mid-
1920s, Dad had a horse billeted with a friend in Washington,
and by the late 1920s his friend, retired Marine Major Harry
Leonard,* was urging Dad to take up horsemanship as a family
sport. This appealed to Dad's sense of family as a loosely
bonded collective, needing authoritative mobilization.

Dad's first horse, Sir Gareth (named, it seemed, for the
Arthurian knight), was soon followed by three more. To my lot
fell a beautiful and gentle brood mare, Maude, coal black and
most civilly conditioned to stop in her tracks when one fell off.

---

*He had served in China in the Boxer Rebellion, where he lost an arm, and
had many tales of exotic and melodramatic experiences.

From left to right: The author, Jane, Dean, and Mary Acheson; we were broken young to the saddle.

To my sister Jane came Miriam, an Arabian mare, a creature of rare grace and speed, chestnut speckled with white flecks, who moved as if made of steel springs. (How an Arabian came by an Old Testament Hebrew name was a mystery that did not concern my innocent young mind.) To Mother came Pilgrim, a powerful, heavy strawberry roan gelding, an Irish hunter, possessed of an iron mouth and a will to match. He was too rough for Mother and was later to do her injury. Pilgrim meant no harm, but was strong, stubborn, and dumb.

Sir Gareth was sold, eventually, and in his place came Katahdin, a retired flat racer, a chestnut gelding with a white star, even-tempered and gentle. He was a sweet horse, well trained and accepting of life as it came. When my sister Mary

Family cavalcade. *From left to right:* The author, Jane, Dean, and Alice
Acheson, circa 1930.

learned to ride, she rode Katahdin, who was led on a halter by
Dad as we formed a family cavalcade.

Twice, Dad took Maude to stud, and from those unions
came two remarkable fillies. Sigrun, the elder of the two, went
to Jane. Miriam was sold. Sigrun was a dark bay with black
points, strong and athletic, "short-barreled" in the rib cage,
spirited, nervous, and spooky. But God made her fly over
jumps, and Jane, an excellent horsewoman, took on the job of
jump training on wing panels in our paddock. She had spectacular results. Sigrun in fact flew over jumps, often with a foot or
more to spare. Wendy, the other filly, two years younger than
Sigrun and from a different sire, came to me as a present from
Dad on condition that I break her to the saddle by my twelfth
birthday. This I was able to do. Wendy, slightly longer-barreled
than Sigrun and marginally less robust, had every bit of Si-

grun's grace and speed, and a slightly diminished measure of Sigrun's temperament. She took to jumps like a bird, but remained skittish and unreliable, sometimes running past the wings. Her beauty and grace endeared her to me, but I could never turn my back on her without fear of a nip on the shoulder, nor did she perform well in show jumping.

But I leap ahead. Long before Jane and I were qualified to jump, we were schooled in basic riding technique by Dad himself. Dad's first tenet was a firm grip with the knees on the saddle girth. He said: "I don't want to see daylight between your knees and the saddle." As our family troop rode along, Dad rode behind Jane and me. Inevitably, our knees would relax and Dad often came cantering up calling, "Daylight, damn it, daylight!" and gave us a smack on the offending knee with his riding crop.

Dad insisted that we learn the full maintenance drill that

Left to right: Mary, Dean, David, and Jane Acheson.

went with horses. After a ride we sponged down the animals and curried their coats, which they visibly enjoyed. We washed the bits and cleaned the saddles and bridle leather with Propert's Saddle Soap, then put them away on pegs in the simple tackhouse next to the barn.

Dad's enthusiasm for riding and horses burned too brightly to burn for very long. One day in early fall, he and Mother and I rode over to the meet of the Howard County Hunt for their first fox hunt of the season, Dad on Sigrun, Mother on Pilgrim, and I on Wendy. When the hounds took the scent and went baying off, the field following, Sigrun caught the spirit of excitement and flew to the front, leaving Mother and me behind. We lost Sigrun and her master for three quarters of an hour. Finally the hounds lost the scent and the whip checked the pack and the field. It was then that Sigrun appeared, riderless, led by her reins held by another rider. Someone went looking for Dad, who was soon found. He was unhurt in body, but grievously wounded in spirit and dignity. He had lost his seat over a fence and landed in a thorn bush, from which he could not extricate himself for the pain inflicted by the thorns upon the slightest movement.

When body had been tested and spirit had been repaired, we hacked our horses back to the farm. The silence was nearly unbroken for the entire ride. I knew better, and Mother certainly did, than to interrupt whatever dark reflections were gathering in Dad's mind. We guessed we were at one of those turning points and that Dad's enthusiasm for our collective equestrian life would never again be the same. We were right.

Independence Day

WHEN MY SISTERS AND I WERE KIDS, let us say from mid-Coolidge to late Hoover eras, my parents spent their summers at their farm, some eighteen miles north of Washington at Sandy Spring, Maryland. I have described this quiet and self-respecting Quaker community dating from the eighteenth century, characterized by civility, sobriety, and community responsibility. We children weeded Mother's flower garden, rode horseback, played with the dog, practiced the piano, and pursued amusements with the few children of our age in the vicinity. One of my most enduring friendships grew from that time and place.

Had I known enough of life to reflect on it, I might have wondered how Dad, son of a British-born Episcopal bishop and fond of vivid individuality in speech, dress, and vocabulary (including that of a field artillery trainee), would work out his relationship with his neighbors in Sandy Spring. In truth, he worked it out very well, being astute enough to know that the question was probably never absent from his neighbors' minds. Mother readily made friends and became active in garden club circles. The most significant cultural challenge was the Fourth of July.

Dad was not a former artilleryman for nothing. To him, Independence Day meant loud noise, gunpowder smoke, and lots of both. We equipped ourselves for that holiday as for a small war, with Chinese string firecrackers, six-inch salutes, cherry bombs, pinwheels, Roman candles, fountains, and sky rockets.

Sloping down to the north from our house was a field of perhaps five acres, running to our neighbor's fence. His land then sloped gently up toward the Quaker Meeting House along the road. These parcels became the Verdun of Independence Day.

Our imaginations started where the manufacturers' left off. Dad was convinced that fireworks manufacturers were too timid to produce a truly satisfying explosion, but that their raw material and our own originality could achieve patriotically satisfying results. Egged on by Dad's enthusiasm, I put to good use an early bent for practical engineering.

From this dubious partnership came at least two formidable creations. One was the two-phase can salvo. At Dad's command we set four or five soup cans on the ground, open end down, each over a cherry bomb—a round, reinforced spherical bomb about an inch and a quarter in diameter. Then we loaded two double-barreled shotguns. We then lit the fuses of the cherry bombs, about two seconds apart. When the fuses burned down, these powerful bombs blew the cans about fifty feet in the air, at two-second intervals. As each can reached its apogee, one of the shotgunners blasted it, kicking it further into the air. This sequence produced loud, rapid-fire reports and a skeetlike test of hand and eye, deeply satisfying to gunners and spectators alike.

Certain hazards were constantly present on July 4. Roman candles had infrequent but unpredictable aberrations, viz., blowing out the bottom of the candle so that the next propulsion would go toward the body instead of skyward. If one were wearing a jacket or long-sleeved shirt, the fiery emission could go up one's sleeve, with serious consequences. The precaution was to hold the Roman candle at a right angle to the axis of the arm. Dad was the safety monitor who enforced this technique.

Another and more frequent hazard was the "sleeper" firecracker. Six-inch salutes seemed particularly prone to burning out the fuse without igniting the firecracker. The standard instruction was: "Light fuse and get away." But after running from the hissing fuse, sometimes nothing would happen. Dad would stop and watch the "sleeper" and, after half a minute, would approach cautiously for a close-up view. This maneuver offered all the security of approaching a motionless rattlesnake. Usually the fuse was out, but sometimes dampness or a tiny defect simply delayed the fuse action and, as Dad came within a few feet, the cracker went off as if actuated by premeditated malice.

One of Dad's pleasing inventions was the sky-rocket/cherry-bomb piggyback. He fastened a cherry bomb or a six-inch salute to the casing of a sky rocket, about halfway along the length of the rocket case, using wire as the fastening because of its non-combustible properties. Then Dad clipped the fuse of the rocket so it was shorter than the fuse of the firecracker. The rocket was placed in a steeply inclined launching trough and both fuses were lighted. The rocket ignited first (having the shorter fuse), carrying the assembled vehicle and payload high into the night sky, whereupon the firecracker or cherry bomb exploded with a deafening report and intense flash.

The artistry lay, of course, in the precision of the timing (and length) of the two fuses. If the payload exploded too early in ascent, much of the drama was lost; similarly, if it exploded as the spent rocket approached the earth. Dad was reasonably expert in the trimming of the two fuses.

The neighbor to the immediate north kept cows in his field, and as the explosions reverberated and the fiery trails shot up over the pasture we sometimes wondered what the effect would be on the taste of July 5 milk production. But if there was unintended offense either to the cows or to the Quaker peace of the neighborhood, we never heard about it. In later years, I came to realize that we had benefited from our neighbors' generous toleration of our eccentricity.

Road Gang

IN THE 1920S AND 1930S, the road from Sandy Spring to the farm—about half a mile—had a McAdam blacktop finish as far as the Quaker Meeting House, about two tenths of a mile. The remaining three tenths of a mile to our gate was gravel and earth. This portion was chronically washed by rain and "washboarded" by use, so that the surface became puddles, ridges, and loose stones emerging from the earth matrix, much of which ran off into the drainage ditch.

Driving on the road in this condition was a physical experience. When the wheels passed over an exposed rock, or hit a gouged-out hole, the rear-seat passengers often hit their heads on the roof and the entire car would shudder. This inspired Dad to fury. "Damn! Damnation!" he would cry as the car reeled from each blow. "We're lucky not to break a spring!" These outbursts presaged the next weekend activity, the road gang.

Dad and I were the permanent members of the road gang. Floaters included my uncle Ted, when he happened to visit, and any young men who came calling on my sister Jane. These were pressed into service so regularly that they soon took to wearing work clothes and boots when they came to the farm for a weekend lunch. Our tools were a long-handled ditch shovel, a couple of heavy mattocks or pickaxes for loosening packed earth, a wheelbarrow, and heavy gloves.

The drill was always the same. Dad's summer job in 1911 as a road hand on the Canadian transcontinental railroad had given him a good mastery of basic roadwork procedure. The rain washed the loose road material into the drainage ditches at the side. Eventually, one had to dig out the ditch, replace the material back on the road, and crown it gently toward the center so that rain would run into the ditch rather than stand in puddles. Repeating the erosion cycle from time to time was obviously inherent in the nature of a gravel road.

At age ten to twelve, wiry and slight of build, I could not inflict much damage with the pickax, but I could shovel out the earth and gravel from the ditch after it was broken up. My favorite role was wheelbarrow driver. I loaded the barrow and wheeled it to the point on the road where the load was to be dropped and spread. Above all, I was proud to be on the team of such a leader.

As we worked, Dad told me stories of the section gang on the railroad, next to whom Bret Harte's characters were gray and commonplace. Dad's tales involved the profane Chinese cook; the one-eyed French Canadian, rumored to have killed a man in a knife fight; the Irish section boss's daughter whose virtue was her father's constant and worrisome concern. Other and lesser characters frequented these reminiscences, all seemingly original and authentic. In the telling, Dad's voice would rise to falsetto (the Chinese cook), drop to enraged basso (the section boss), assume a comical "Canuck" accent (the knife fighter), accompanied by a popping of the eyes and extravagant gestures of the hands. He played all the parts with skill born of much practice (as I later learned from his closest friends). He never felt a story had to be an affidavit.

After two or three weekends of toil, even the worst parts of the road were restored to good shape and the ditches deep and clean. Then we got in the car with my mother and sisters and Dad drove a demonstration lap up the road and back. "What about that? Smooth as silk. Not one damn bump!" and, "The road gang did it again!" His reward was a tangible result and the knowledge of a good job.

To me the reward was more material. Since the road gang usually worked on a weekend, we could look forward to a generous and tasty weekend lunch. We walked back to the house and washed up. Dad went to the kitchen and addressed the cook. The badinage was pretty predictable: "Laura, you've got two starved laborers for lunch. What are you going to feed us?"

"Well, Mr. Acheson, I've got jellied consommé for the first course, then for the main course I've got fried chicken, succotash, riced potatoes with gravy, and collard greens. For dessert, vanilla ice cream, chocolate sauce, and pound cake."

"Doesn't sound like enough, but we'll make it do."

(Much laughter over this well-rehearsed exchange.)

After a huge lunch we dozed or read for an hour and then walked back to work on the road. The calories soon vanished and by five o'clock we were hungry again. Then we piled the tools in the wheelbarrow and wheeled it back to the toolshed.

Walking back, Dad sometimes said: "You know, some day we'll have to black-top the damn road. Then we'll have a smooth road and no more fun." He laughed over the irony and his own uncertainty over which objective he really wanted.

Murray Bay, Equalizer Tennis, and the Debutante of the Year

■■■■■■■■■■■■■■

URING THE MID-1930S, Dad hit upon Murray Bay as a promising venue for a family summer vacation. Murray Bay was a pleasant summer colony in the province of Quebec, near the junction of the Saguenay and St. Lawrence rivers. One of the great Canadian Pacific Railroad hotels had been built there, the Manoir Richelieu, and not far away a turn-of-the-century summer settlement of cottages had been established, occupying several terrace levels up from the floodplain. The summer residents were well-to-do, but generally not fancy, people from Montreal, Boston, Cincinnati, New York, and a few from Washington. In this last category was Miss Mabel Boardman, who had recommended Murray Bay to my parents. Senator Robert A. Taft and his family had a house there which supplied several attractive and pleasant children of the ages of my sisters and me. There was a nucleus of a dozen or more boys and girls my age (fifteen to eighteen). The summer of 1939 was our last summer there and this vignette is placed in that year.

The pleasures of Murray Bay were wholesome, but not marked by variety or originality. Picnic outings were the standard social format, usually evening affairs in a rocky field, where the evening chill would be relieved by a blazing fire and group singing. Golf, tennis (my sport), and fishing outings were standard daytime diversions. The first two were played at the rather simple Murray Bay Golf Club. A few families had private tennis courts. One of these belonged to the parents of my friend Phil.

Mother and Dad afforded me considerable license where tennis was concerned and I used it to exempt myself from command family activities. Phil was a creditable player and similarly sought a bit of *lebensraum* for himself. We would talk, play a set, talk, play a set, and so on for much of the day. We discovered in each other a speculative cast of mind, and soon turned the spotlight of analysis on an interesting problem.

Golf is played with handicaps, so that two ill-matched players can play each other with reasonably interesting competition. Why did tennis not evolve in the same way? Club tennis was awkward in that one could not pick up a decent game with just anyone. Club pros worked hard to set up matches between fairly even players, but often none were available. Surely there was a remedy for this obtuse oversight.

One day Phil and I hit on it. Suppose, we said, the winner of the first game took a half-ounce sip of whiskey at the change of serve. Then someone would win the second game. He would take a half ounce of whiskey, and so on it would go. If the same winner won four to five games in a row, he would take aboard enough whiskey to impair his superiority. But his opponent would not gain a lasting advantage because, for every game he won, he would have to drink whiskey. It seemed to us that, whatever the initial advantage, the players would sooner or later equalize the difference in skill, perhaps not in a set as short as six games, but surely in a longer set of, say, sixteen or twenty games. Theoretically, all advantage would succumb to whiskey, so that scores could run to 100–all or higher. We resolved to test the theory that afternoon, in a limited experiment of sixteen games.

Phil's parents' bar provided a bottle of Gooderham & Wortz* Canadian whiskey, and we started out. My initial advantage, being slight, was pretty well equalized by the third or fourth game, by which time I had taken two ounces of straight whiskey. Then Phil started catching up. Before he could establish a clear ascendancy, the whiskey started catching up with him. By 6–all we were still playing but the errors were now frequent and evenly distributed. By 8–all we had reached the limit of our sixteen-game experiment. Inebriation and the approach of the dinner hour were clinching arguments that we stop.

I made it on foot to my parents' rented cottage not far away, barely before the dinner hour. Dad regarded me with surprise and distaste, perspiring as I was, none too clean, and not certain where or how to place my feet. The symptoms were not mysterious to him. "Where have you been and what have you been doing?" he demanded. "I've been playing equalizer tennis with Phil," said I. "What in the hell is equalizer tennis?" he asked. Then: "Don't tell me. I think I know." I started

---

*A brand founded by Dad's maternal family, the Gooderhams, and sold out to Hiram Walker in Edwardian times.

upstairs to wash and change. "Either change for dinner or go to bed, but do one or the other in five minutes," he called after me. Bed felt good, and dinner I didn't need or want.

Looking back, I can see that our family's summers at Murray Bay, being concentrated in my pre-college years, came at an unsettled time of life for me. While the inner man claimed adulthood, common sense and emotional maturity fell far short of such a claim. This was a source of constant striving to demonstrate *savoir faire* and sophistication, never so great as in the presence of girls. I had read Booth Tarkington's *Seventeen,* but was unable or unwilling to recognize myself.

The girls at Murray Bay were attractive and friendly, and some of them had been friends of two or three earlier summers. Being well-mannered, considerate young ladies, they were not, generally speaking, out to aggravate panic in a seventeen-year male. One was an exception, so remote and so glamorous that all self-assurance fled in her presence. She was the Debutante of the Year (I will call her DOTY to protect the innocent), which is to say that she became the following winter the most celebrated debutante of the year and perhaps of all time in the nation, her picture even on the cover of *Time* Magazine. She made her debut at a great splash of a party given by her mother and stepfather in New York, the likes of which had not been seen since the days of the robber barons. She was very pale, dramatically brunette, with quizzical eyebrows and the manner of one who had seen everything and everyone of any consequence. And she was here in Murray Bay, provincial little Murray Bay! I had to meet her, and set about engineering an introduction, which was duly arranged.

The receiving line at the Washington Debutante Ball, December 1965. *Left to right:* David C. Acheson, Jr., Mrs. Paul H. Nitze (partially obscured), Dean Acheson, Eleanor Dean Acheson (giving her grandfather the word), and Eleanor's friend Sandra Auchincloss. FREUDY PHOTOS

My parents took different views of my interest in DOTY. While my mother thought that social intercourse between the sexes was a necessary and desirable path to civilization of the young male, Dad saw this case as a comic rite, like the mating dance of the Sandhill Crane.

At the very end of the summer there was a picnic supper for all of our age, and by luck and early application I persuaded DOTY to go with me. Our family's transportation at that period consisted of two cars, a black convertible 120 h.p. Packard which my sister Jane and I were free to use, and a seven-passenger Buick limousine which was for full family loads and my parents' social outings. We had driven to Murray Bay from Washington in a two-car caravan, Jane and I in the Packard and the others in the Buick. The Packard was to be my transportation to the picnic with DOTY; a few days later our caravan was to drive the first leg toward Washington. It was important to make a favorable final impression on DOTY. I picked her up in the Packard late on a fine afternoon and we started off.

All the roads at Murray Bay were gravel, some worn to washboard worse than others. Our course initially lay downhill from the second terrace to the bottom level, then a right turn to the picnic ground a few miles away. As I approached the bottom, I braked slightly to go into the right turn. Another car was coming from the right, turning left up the hill that I had descended. We were on parallel tracks. As I braked, the Packard slid sideways to the left a few feet, the gravel too loose to hold tight traction. Just before I heard the crunch of metal, I recognized the other car. It was my parents' Buick. My father was driving, and in the car were my mother and grandmother. Then the crunch. Both cars stopped and we got out.

What had happened was a one-in-a-million freak accident. As my Packard slid toward the oncoming Buick, nearly side by side, the very tip of the rear bumper of the Buick caught the front fender of my car, peeling off the front fender, the running board, and the rear fender of the Packard. All three pieces were surgically removed as a single unit. Not a mark appeared on the Buick anywhere.

Standing there at the side of the gravel road, Dad's manner was one of grim, calm rage, and his comments much to the point. "That car," pointing at the Packard, "must be driven to Washington. You will stay here and get it fixed. If you can't get it fixed, drive it into the river. Whether you go in with it is entirely up to you." I looked over to see how DOTY was taking all this. She had gone. No one saw her leave.

Jane was marvelous. The two of us took the Packard in to the local mechanic, who came and collected the loose hardware lying on the road. Jane's French, polished by an earlier summer with one Mme de Salle du Pin in Paris, was equal to making a reasonable deal with the rustic Québecois mechanic. Repairs were done in a couple of days and we made our long journey home to Washington without incident. When we arrived home, nothing further was said about the accident. Dad was a believer in "least said, sooner mended," applicable to people and cars.

DOTY went on to fame and glory.

Uncle Ted and
the Hornets

B EFORE UNCLE TED, my father's brother, was married,
he used to visit us at the farm fairly frequently. Ted
was one of my two godfathers and a hero of my
adolescent years. He was nine years younger than Dad, tall,
vivid in speech and manners. His hair was curly and blond,
truly gold, matched by a blond mustache with a rakish twist at
the ends. He was full of jokes and wit, had a bizarre sense of
humor and a line of charming, amusing patter which he lavished on ladies and children.

Ted was a true product of the Roaring Twenties. Few who
knew him at Williams College could forget his dramatic progress around the campus in a yellow Stutz Bearcat, German
student cap, and raccoon coat. After college he broke horses
and shot mountain sheep in British Columbia, then worked as
a reporter on the city desk of the *Hartford Courant.* This led to
literary aspirations. He moved to England for a few years, wrote
and published half a dozen detective stories, and took up study
at the London School of Economics. There he took a Ph.D. in
the mid-1930s. Ted was very bright and temperamentally rest-

less. To master "the dismal science" must have been a great effort of personal discipline for him.

Later, Ted taught a course called Money and Banking at George Washington University, where he became a lecturer of legendary popularity. His annual lecture on currency arbitrage was always a sensation.

Edward C. Acheson, Jr. (Uncle Ted), as a young blade.

Dad enjoyed Ted (as who did not?), but managed to convey an older brother's—and a lawyer's—impatience with what he saw as Ted's harum-scarum life. This tended to provoke in Ted even more unconventional behavior, and so the cycle would mount, each proffering his counter-example, but unheeded.

Occasionally Dad expanded upon Ted and the Acheson roots. Dad spoke of the "wild Ulster streak" that his father had, and saw it amply manifested in Ted. In later life I speculated that Dad's real concern was that the "wild Ulster streak" might surface in himself at an inopportune time and belie the disciplined, analytical lawyer. Yet what distinguished Dad, for the better, from other disciplined, analytical lawyers was precisely the "wild Ulster streak." It made him imaginative, vehement, an effective advocate, not averse to risk, and a larger-than-life person.

But I digress. Ted was with us at the farm in the mid-thirties, recovering from the removal of his appendix. Perhaps thirty yards from the farmhouse was the antique engraving

The guest house, Harewood Farm, home of the hornets.

shop converted into a guest house—a clapboard building consisting of one story, a huge bedroom with a high ceiling, and a more recently added bath wing. At one end of the main structure, over several seasons, a hive of hornets had built and enlarged their characteristic papier-mâché nest under the apex of the eaves of the roof. These bees were the large, gray-green, white-faced, irritable and highly venomous breed that take no prisoners and do not countenance disturbance by a mere property owner. I knew them well and gave them a wide berth. An occasional guest had been stung. Ted was now living in the guest house. He broached the subject of exterminating the hornets.

Full of charm and guile, Ted put it up to me. Surely I would like a position of trust in a bold enterprise that would rid us of the hornets? I was afraid of the hornets, but more afraid of disappointing Uncle Ted. We discussed several scenarios. The most definitive appeared to be controlled fire. Suppose we got a long pole of plaster lathing from the barn, wired rags to the end, doused them with kerosene, and lit them? We would hold it close under the nest; the hornets would emerge; their wings would be singed away. While the nest structure might remain, the inhabitants would perish.

Ted and I agreed to try the scenario on Dad. He was not enthusiastic. "Brilliant, brilliant!" he said. "Of course the fire engines won't get here until the guest house is gone. Then my insurance claim is out the window because you geniuses tried to torch the place. I have to go to my office this morning, but you need a better idea than this." He admonished us to do nothing until he returned to the farm, but to think about it.

When Dad had gone, Ted and I put our minds to work. I was mechanically ingenious to a tolerable degree and Ted was one to go all out. This dangerous combination evolved a plan.

At the barn we found strips of lathing twenty to twenty-five feet in length, enough to reach the hornet stronghold. We also found baling wire and burlap sacks. It was not difficult to fashion a hoop of wire, fasten the open mouth of a sack to the hoop, and fasten the crude assembly to the end of the strip of lathing. Then we put newspaper in the outdoor trash incinerator nearby and set it alight.

Moving in under the hornet nest, we raised the pole until the open hoop was around the nest, lifted it to the edge of the eaves, and gave a sharp pull against the nest where it attached to the eaves. The nest dropped into the sack. We turned the pole over twice, closing the mouth of the sack, and carried our prize a few yards to the blazing incinerator. Hornets and sack went up in a searing blaze. One or two hornets escaped, but did not succeed in fixing responsibility upon Ted and me. They flew about for a while in an aimless rage.

About six o'clock in the evening Dad returned to the farm from town. Ted and I decided to play it cool. Dad made a Martini and then took the home front under review. "How did you guys do with the bees?" "Come and see," we replied. Dad came with us to the east end of the guest house and looked up. Where the hornets' military base had hung, the veritable Gwalior or Riga of hornet fortification, there was only a stub of nest material still stuck to the eaves.

We described our procedure to Dad. As we talked, he broke into his familiar wolfish grin, front teeth prominent, mustache pulled back, eyes sparkling with amusement. "Pretty damn neat," he said. The wild Ulster streak had some uses, after all.

Duffy and Domestic Disorder

D AMN! THERE'S THAT BLASTED DOG AGAIN, making an infernal racket!" Dad's voice drifted through the house in the early morning hours, the middle of a warm, still summer night at the farm. Minutes later, my sister's soft tread could be heard on the stairs, going down to the backyard to bring Duffy in and shelter him from Dad's wrath. Duffy, a gray giant Schnauzer, was amusing himself by tearing up a cardboard carton under the house, indeed making an infernal racket.

Duffy came to us by the intervention of Uncle Ted. Ted had lived for a number of years in rural England, where he had kept dogs, having a particular fondness for giant Schnauzers. Ted had urged Dad to get a dog and Dad, for better or worse, put the matter in Ted's hands. Duffy duly appeared, big, good-natured, possessed of nervous, indiscriminate, random energy. Duffy returned affection readily, but seemed resistant to instruction. He swung between being highly distractible and totally preoccupied with his own agenda of the moment. There could hardly have been two more antithetical temperaments and intellects than Dad's and Duffy's. Duffy was to Dad what anti-matter is to matter. Dad mistook intellectual obtuseness for willful defiance, as he tended to do with people. Duffy took Dad's irritation for hostility. They were fated for conflict.

Since we lived on a farm of seemingly ample acreage, Duffy was first allowed to run loose. He could not get into much trouble on the property. Our farm animals—horses and cattle—were intimidating to Duffy, but could do him no harm as long as he sat outside the pasture fence and barked, which he did much of the time. But in the manner of dogs, Duffy's explorations of his own territory eventually became boring to him, and inevitably he cast his eye upon Mr. Snowden's neighboring farm.

Mr. Snowden kept chickens. They were not regularly penned and often ran loose in the house yard and fields, and along the road. Duffy discovered the pleasing panic-proneness of chickens. When chased, they squawked and flapped and made a lot of commotion, running in erratic course, but not too fast. Frightened chickens invited chase. The chase invited the kill. In a very short time Duffy became a chicken-killer. When the accusation was first brought to Dad by Mr. Snowden, Dad was incredulous, then furious. His standing in the community was being tarnished by no act of his own. He had been betrayed by "man's best friend." He promised to pay for the deceased chickens and to cure the problem at its source.

Somewhere—perhaps in his Connecticut youth—Dad had heard of a sure-shot cure for a chicken-killer. The remedy was to take the corpse of the most recent victim and tie it around the neck of the offending beast. In theory, the chicken would become so offensive in decay that the dog would never want anything to do with chickens again. This notion appealed to

Dad for two reasons: it was a constructive, remedial punishment, and it afforded a use for the chicken that Dad had to pay for anyway. So the newest victim was tied to Duffy's collar with heavy twine. "We'll give that idiot dog a heavy dose of his own medicine," was Dad's pronouncement of judgment.

True to his perverse form, however, Duffy failed to follow Dad's prescription. It was short work for Duffy to tear the dead chicken from his collar and devour it. This done, it was natural for him to see the entire transaction as a reward for a successful hunt, and to go forth and repeat his offense. Now Duffy's owners were no longer part of law enforcement, but were accomplices. A new and less oblique deterrent was devised. Duffy was tied to a long clothesline lead, which was snapped, as a runner, to another length of clothesline tied between two trees. Thus Duffy could run about for some distance, but could not run away.

Ever resourceful, Duffy found new means of entertainment. The lead, running for fifteen to twenty yards between the two trees, afforded him access to the trash pile in the shed near the kitchen. There he found large cardboard grocery cartons, carried them under the kitchen, and rended them with ferocious growls and primitive tearing noises. It was this game that intruded on Dad's sleep in the dead of night.

Late in the summer Mother and Dad and the family went off on a vacation trip, leaving Ted in charge of the farm and of Duffy. Dad's parting admonition to Ted was: "You brought this damn animal into our lives. See if you can teach him some sense." For some weeks we vacationed in a cooler place, unmindful of Duffy, returning shortly before school was to open. Ted was triumphant, and couldn't wait to show us what Duffy had learned in our absence. "Now watch him," said Ted. "I will say *à la place!*" With this there was a scramble of paws on a wood floor and Duffy dove under the skirt of the sofa, then we saw eyes and nose peering out from beneath the skirt to see how we were taking this new achievement. "He's really smart," said Ted. "You just have to know how to teach him." Dad was not appreciative. "Just what we need, Ted. A crazy dog that speaks French, with a knack for parlor tricks."

Eventually Ted was good enough to adopt Duffy and take him off our hands. "Poetic justice" was Dad's epitaph on this close of the Duffy episode.

The Well-Dressed Man

THERE COULD BE NO QUESTION that Dad was a thorough, unreconstructed dude, a fashionplate. This was true from as early as any of his family can remember. An early photograph of him and Mother in the Acheson garden in Middletown, Connecticut, shows him in full cutaway regalia—spats, tailcoat, gray vest, etc.—perhaps in connection with a service at his father's church. As children, my sisters and I were taken each Christmas morning to call on Mrs. Chapin (a distinguished Washington widow), a ceremonial visit for which Dad put on a gray Ascot, cutaway tailcoat, striped black and gray trousers, dove gray spats, and black shoes shined to a reflective luster. This was his dress for the entire holiday, regardless of weather. A tall shiny-silk top hat, Chesterfield overcoat, and dove gray gloves completed his equipage for outdoor expeditions on Christmas Day. A vivid memory of Christmas Day, 1946 or '47, was of Dad, so attired, sliding on the ice on P Street with some black children from the next block.

On informal occasions, Dad's dress was no less meticulous. For the office he was likely to favor a gray, or brown, or slate blue or navy suit, often double-breasted. His taste in shirts ran to stripes with detachable stiff white collar (short, spread points) and French cuffs with small gold cufflinks carrying his engraved monogram in a graceful, cursive script. He liked figured ties rather than stripes and viewed a striped tie with a striped shirt as a solecism betraying a lack of instruction. Sometimes Dad wore a tweed suit to his law office. One I recall vividly was a rust color, of a small herringbone pattern. This was worn with a brown figured tie, striped shirt with short white collar, brown socks (always mid-calf with garters), and smooth calf brown shoes polished to the usual gleam.

Button-down shirts did not come into vogue until the 1930s. When they did, Dad took to them, preferring plain white, but never wore them with a blue suit or sober business wear.

It was not vanity, I thought and still think, which prompted Dad to lavish great care on his dress. Rather, it was one of many manifestations of a perfectionist drive that touched everything he did. His aesthetic sense was sharp. It would have offended that sense to put on clothes that in their cut, style, color combination, and condition could not have withstood the most critical scrutiny.

A variable in Dad's preparations in presenting himself to the world was the question of the handkerchief. Should it pick up the dominant color in the necktie, or in the shirt, or perhaps the white of the collar? Reasonable men could differ on this issue and Dad went different ways at different times. He had, as indeed he must, a vast array of handkerchiefs representing nearly every shade of every color, so that it was highly improbable that a shirt or a tie would not find an appropriate response in the handkerchief. They were all neatly folded and ironed, and kept in a drawer in a graduated, spectrumlike order of color.

In 1965, when I was a senior official in the Treasury, a colleague, Stanley Surrey, told me of a meeting he (representing the government) had with Dad during the 1930s, involving a tax litigation. As Stan described it, while the meeting progressed, Stan's eye became bemused by Dad's sartorial perfection, traveling over the finished worsted brown herringbone suit, his brown and white figured tie, a tan shirt with white stiff collar, a handkerchief which picked up in its field the color of the shirt and in its border the dominant color of the tie, dark brown socks, and medium brown shoes so polished that the furniture was reflected. Stan lost himself in an analysis of each detail and pondered the formidable degree of forethought that the ensemble must require. This led Stan to contemplate the degree of forethought that Dad must have lavished on a far more serious matter, the litigation at hand. This, in turn, led Stan's mind to the likelihood that such forethought had built a strong case and how this could affect the result of the litigation. Afterwards, one of Stan's colleagues asked him what the substance of the meeting was. "I haven't the slightest idea," Stan replied. "I was totally absorbed in my study of Mr. Acheson's symphony in brown, and its implications."

Several times during my teens I was encouraged to accompany Dad to his tailor, a block or two from his office at 15th and H streets (Northwest) in Washington. These sessions were instructive, for it became apparent at once that Dad was no mere passive tailor's client, but had considerable technical command of the subject. Dad liked both double- and single-breasted jacket styles and always had some suits of each, leaning more to single-breasted in the post–World War II era and more to double-breasted prewar. He liked very little padding in the shoulder, and no vent in the tail of the jacket. Always his trousers were cuffed, except for dress clothes. He liked buttonholes at the buttons on the jacket sleeve, either three or four. He

Dean Acheson in sporty dress, with Alice Acheson, Bermuda, 1951. (How often does one see a three-piece tweed suit with a straw hat?) ACME PHOTO

hated a lot of shirt cuff showing. Every visit to the tailor involved a bit of bullying to make the sleeve longer than the tailor wanted, if left to himself.

The waist of the jacket had to be shaped—not pinched, but with just the suggestion of a tapered waist. One of Dad's real peeves was the tendency of tailors to cut the jacket collar too shallow so that an inch or more of shirt collar emerged above the collar of the jacket. Dad always made sure the tailor understood this was not a discretionary matter. "Raise the damn collar—I'm not advertising shirt linen." The tailor would raise his tape another three quarters of an inch up the neck.

In Dad's normal standing posture, the calves of his legs thrust back against the trousers, just enough to elevate slightly the back of the trouser cuff. Thus, when viewed from the side, his trouser cuff was not horizontal. It irritated Dad that his body was working against his aesthetic sense. A sly treachery was at work. It was the tailor's job to put down this subversion. "I'm not a college sophomore, God damn it, and I'm not selling socks. I want the cuffs cut on a slight slant, down toward the back." The tailor explained patiently that he could easily slope uncuffed trousers, but trouser cuffs had to be perpendicular to the vertical line of the trousers, otherwise there would be a stress in the sewn cuff. Dad thought this was a mere excuse for laziness. "Nonsense. Anything you can cut on the horizontal you can cut on a slant."

The next fitting was always an interesting session. If the tailor had decided that Dad's departures from standard practice were ill-advised and that possibly his client would not notice corrections, the fitting became a criminal court. Accusations of betrayal were followed by pleas in extenuation. Stan-

dard practice was best. Surely Mr. Acheson would not want to
be thought eccentric. By the end of the first fitting, the tailor's
spirit was broken. At the final fitting, all disagreement was past
history. Dad viewed the work as his own in every detail, almost
purring with satisfaction, seeing in each nuance a victory of eye
and brain, his aesthetic sense at peace with itself.

When I first became aware of these things, Dad was going
to an excellent tailor, D'Elia & Marks Co. near his office. For
haberdashery, he went to Sidney West & Co., whose label
carried a half-sun symbol (presumably a setting one), and to
Brooks Brothers in New York. Later, in the 1950s, the favorite
tailor was Farnsworth-Reed until they moved to a garish shop-
ping mall in suburban Virginia. Concurrently Dad patronized
J. Press & Co. in New Haven, when he went each month to
that city for meetings of the Yale Corporation. In the 1930s
Dad had shoes made to his measurements by Peal & Co. in
London, but their prices went beyond his means in the postwar
years. He discovered that Peal made shoes in stock for Brooks
Brothers, to be sold readymade, and until his death he found
this resource suited his taste and his purse very well.

Clothes to Dad were never a mere self-indulgence. Rather,
they were the skin he put on to reflect the personality beneath—crisp, harmonious, bold but not quite flamboyant, a
challenge to perfection in the last detail.

Away from civilization at the farm, Dad dressed for dinner
with family and friends in a fashion for which outrageous
would be an understatement. Summer dinner costume, often
as not, was a pleated cotton wedding shirt from Mexico or the
islands, lime green slacks, no socks, sandals or Mexican *huara-
ches* on the feet, an orange sash around the waist falling to the

knee. He had the panache of the portrait of Trelawny by Lawrence, without the turban. To his family it did not require
explanation that his *outré* dress supplied a release from the pent-
up pressures of conformity and made it easier for him to act and
dress the Washington lawyer (or, later, the statesman) when he
was on stage. His family often tested the limits of outrageousness
by giving him articles of dress that even he might think went too
far. But it became clear there were no limits. Green Belgian
shoes, pink elephant socks, printed cotton slacks, underwear
with red ants pictured thereon—none of these produced any
response from Dad but delight.

Domestic Tranquility

C ONSTANT CURRENTS in Dad's life were the pleasure
and pain he derived from his uneven relationships
with the small domestic staff that he and Mother
employed from the time I was a small child. The core staff were
two: a cook and a houseman, or butler, who doubled as driver or
"chauffeur," the elegant term of choice at that time. There was
sometimes also a laundress who came in by the day, and extra
help for an occasional dinner party.

In the very early days, before my parents employed a couple, there was a succession of single women whose jurisdiction
moved between the kitchen and child care with imprecision
befitting their lack of any noticeable skill in either department.
Dad's father, as Episcopal Bishop of Connecticut, took an interest in an institution of that state that sought to rehabilitate
young wayward women. The bishop thought that working for
my parents would start these delinquents down the right path
and at the same time satisfy my parents' requirements for help.
As we lived in Washington, these ladies came to us sight un-
seen, except by my grandparents. I remember nothing particularly untoward, but learned later that one of these parolees, so

to speak, took me along on a date with her boyfriend, inspiring temporary panic in my parents and the District of Columbia police. I thought nothing of it. Early recollections are kaleidoscopic, and it was not until Johnson and his wife, Laura, came to work that our domestic help became personalities to me.

Dad liked things to go well in the house. He was never indulgent about glitches. If meals were late or badly cooked, or the laundry mishandled, he became irritable. Laura was a good cook, and before long that department was a source of

Edward Youter Johnson: Butler, chauffeur, counselor, mixologist, and friend.

contentment to him rather than of anxiety.

From the start, Johnson and Dad hit it off. Johnson, or more fully, Edward Youter Johnson, was within a few months of Dad's age. He had the gift of innate, unruffled, and kindly dignity. He was good-humored, handsome, even and calm in speech and manner. These were all qualities that Dad found restful. Johnson laughed at Dad's jokes and made himself helpful and agreeable in countless ways, mainly by just being Johnson.

Johnson was thorough and deliberate to a fault. When he started something—shining Dad's shoes, or preparing cocktails in the evening—he followed a step-by-step cycle which no one could hasten. It took as long as it had to take. Dad: "When are we going to see those cocktails, Johnson?" Johnson: "Well, I just put in the gin. Then I got to put in the Vermouth, chill the glasses, and shake the mix with ice. Then I put in the olive, put the whole thing on a tray. Then you get your cocktail." Tie score. No one succeeded in hurrying Johnson or in rattling him, and he never sought to score points. In any proffered criticism or admonition, the ball ended where it started—on the line of scrimmage.

During the school year we children had supper in the kitchen, graduating in turn to dine with our parents at about age ten. During supper in the kitchen, Johnson and I talked a lot about cars, in which I took an early interest. Johnson owned an Essex sedan, my parents a Studebaker. Johnson expanded on the fine points of the Essex; never any criticism of the Studebaker. I undertook to sell my father on turning in the Studebaker and getting an Essex. Dad spoke of the good points of the Studebaker; not a bad word about the Essex. I could see that this was a much more complex matter than I thought, not by any means confined to the merits of cars. They were the players, I just the scoreboard.

When summer came and we moved to the farm, with school forgotten for three months, Johnson became my companion, as well as butler and chauffeur, no doubt with Dad's encouragement. Johnson was partial to float-fishing for sun perch in the nearby Patuxent River, so we often repaired there with a can of worms easily spaded from the barn yard. Sitting on the bank, Johnson concentrated on the teaser nibbles, which he interpreted as confidence-building measures by the fish. Then a big one pulled the bobber down, a gentle yank, and we had a fish. We often got half a dozen or more. Over a picnic lunch, Johnson discussed things that needed fixing at the farm, the wasps' nest in the convertible roof of the family car, the woeful state of the road from the farm to the Quaker Meeting House, and occasionally dropped gentle hints that some recent transaction with my parents had ended unfairly from Johnson's point of view. I was not expected to intervene in these matters. Johnson was preparing my cast of mind for a much later day.

Dad always reacted in a gratifying way to the catch we brought home, a few half-pound sun perch and sometimes a catfish. Dad to the cook: "Laura, the fishermen brought our breakfast for tomorrow. We won't starve after all." This was for Johnson's benefit as much as for mine. Laura fried the fish with breadcrumbs for breakfast, and we speculated that we could survive on sun perch if the Great Depression forced us to that.

Domestic tranquility was shattered some years later when an issue arose between Mother and Laura which prompted Mother to let Johnson and Laura go. They had been hired as a couple and as a couple they had to go. Dad was horrified, but faced with a fait accompli. For Dad and Mother, that was the beginning of more than a decade of a revolving door.

One of Johnson's innumerable successors, one John, was to make his mark indelibly in Dad's memory by a frustrating combination—incorrigible neglect of duty coupled with sincere and heart-tugging remorse which, in John's view, wiped the slate clean. A striking case comes to mind. John drove from the farm into Washington on a Sunday off and "tied one on" in a major way. Upon his return, fearful of waking the house in his condition, he stretched out in the back of his car in the shed and went to sleep. In the morning Dad woke at his usual Monday hour, dressed, and went downstairs. No John. No breakfast. No sign of life. Dad went looking for John and found him at his place of rest. "John, get in the house at once, put on your white coat and get breakfast on the table." John hastily complied. As Dad was finishing breakfast, still before 8:00 A.M., and was about to drive to his office in town, he heard a familiar sound in the pantry, of ice, liquid, glass, and silver. John entered the dining room bearing a small silver tray. On it was a delicately stemmed glass, frost covering the outside but not quite concealing the cold, colorless liquid within. It was John's remorse offering. He spoke. "Mr. Acheson, would you-all like a Martini?" Dad recognized the part he was called upon to play in this sacrifice. "Why, thank you John." He drank it on the spot. Once more the slate was clean.

Johnson returned to my parents' employ not many years after the war, alone. He had separated from Laura. He had run a Washington bachelor house during the war, as major domo. That house was undergoing a heavy turnover of occupants, which, coupled with Dad's blandishments, brought Johnson back. Both parties saw it as a renewal of a fated partnership. To Dad, it meant that the household would once more be predictable—not necessarily efficient, but ordered and smooth.

Not many years after Johnson's return, Dad was nominated

Dean Acheson with his family after his swearing in as Secretary of State, 1949. *Left to right:* Patricia C. Acheson, Mary Acheson Bundy, Alice Acheson, Dean Acheson, David C. Acheson, and Jane Acheson Brown.

to be Secretary of State. His confirmation hearing was noisy and controversial, but the Senate vote was heavily favorable (83–6). Dad returned to his Georgetown house that January evening and handed Johnson his hat, coat, and gloves. "Well, Johnson, the Senate confirmed me today by a vote of 83 to 6. What do you think of that?" Johnson understood that a complimentary response was called for to recognize this milestone, but had no idea what the context was. He played it safe. "Mr.

Acheson, the way I see it, that other fella just wasted his time runnin'." This *bon mot* quickly made its way around town.

In the 1920s and 1930s, there was a farmhouse on the property immediately south of our farm. Its occupant was a highly respected and self-reliant black man named—truly—Sam Hill. Every day he drove a horse and buggy from his house, past our farm, up to the Sandy Spring Store and post office, or to church. I often saw him, roof down, straw hat on his head and another on his black horse's head, moving at a trot along the rutted country road that abutted our barn and hay field. He was a serious man, all business, courteous but brisk. Sam and his remarkable wife had about a dozen children, fairly evenly divided between the sexes. With trivial exceptions these children, closely spaced in age and all young adults at this period, were smart, hardworking, and agreeable. For a few years they provided all of the field help on our small farm and much of the extra help in the house.

The Hill males were particularly active on our behalf when corn and wheat were to be harvested and the timothy cut, dried, and gathered for hay. There was a large hayloft in our ancient barn. The hay was raked into rows in the field by a horse-drawn rake which sometimes I was allowed to operate. One drove the horse forward until the hay pulled along by the rake was even with the row laid down by the last lap of the rake. Then one pulled on an iron lever near the seat. The rake teeth (actually curved combs perhaps thirty-six inches in length) would neatly drop the hay so as to extend the row laid down by the previous passage of the machine.

The Hills often let me ride the hay wagon. There was a magic moment when the horses drew the fully loaded wagon toward the open great barn door. The wagon was filled with hay right up to the jamb at the top of the door. If I remained on the wagon, I would be scraped off as the wagon passed under the jamb. The trick was so slide off the rear edge of the load inches ahead of the approaching jamb. This was exciting for me and highly entertaining for the Hills. I would wait until cries of apprehension from the Hills told me that the last ounce of drama had been exploited, then drop to the ground.

The Hills, men and women, were competent singers. At work in the fields, the men sang spirituals and other songs well known in the rural black community. For my benefit, when I was in the fields with them, they often sang "Oh, little David, play on your harp," a lively spiritual with a rhythmic chorus. Dad sometimes engaged the Hills to sing for summer dinner guests. After dinner we walked up to the barn, each carrying a chair, and listened to the melodic and moving music on the loading floor of the barn. The acoustics were not bad and we were safe from the rain.

About midway in our life on the farm, Dad hired a new tenant farmer. The old farmer's house on our property in the woods was decayed beyond repair. Dad had a small house, tidy but modern, built for Joe and his family. Joe and Dad became nearly as close as Dad and Johnson, and often worked side by side, repairing fences, digging postholes and the like. For Dad, the lessons of the section gang in Canada still applied—equal work carried equal status. While he was digging postholes he answered, as Joe did, to their common boss, who looked like Dad, but wore a different hat. One day, the labor and the hot summer sun began to tell on Dad's years, and he had to put the posthole digger down. "Joe, I have to rest. You're a better man than I am." Joe replied: "Well, I just *got* to be." No answer could be made.

Perhaps the low point in domestic tranquility came in the early postwar years, before Johnson's return, when Mother and Dad were away on a vacation trip and my sister Jane and her husband were in charge of the farm. The domestic couple then in residence carried on a rich emotional life of frequent spats and much dramatic escalation on both sides. This always spilled over onto job performance, and once too often. Jane, an erstwhile Navy wife and (early in life) a student government leader, had a low tolerance for nonsense and fired the couple on the spot. A few days later Mother and Dad returned to find a note from their daughter, by then departed: "Dear Mother and Dad: While you were away I had to fire the help. Will explain later. Love, Jane." "Good God," said Dad, and went to the liquor closet for relief from this unanticipated stress. There was a note there also. "Dear Dad: I thought it best to hide the key to the liquor closet. Will explain later. Love, Jane." By now Dad was Job's direct descendant. "Good God, Alice. We have no help and no liquor." Mother calmly pointed out that the nearby Olney Inn was still serving.

Following Johnson's return, an early tradition was revived, and Johnson, like the legendary cymbalist, lived for his big moment of the year. This came in June, preceded by Dad's quiet announcement: "Johnson, next Friday we are having our mint julep party. Please have it all ready well ahead of time." Johnson worked in stages. Stage one—D minus three days— was to find the large terra cotta crock, wash it, and pour in a quantity of Bourbon whiskey—two or three bottles. Mint was crushed and added, with powdered sugar. The crock was covered and allowed to sit in the basement until D-Day. That morning, silver mugs were placed in the refrigerator to acquire a heavy frost. By then, some mysterious chemistry had worked an impressive change in the contents of the crock. From potent they had become lethal. At H-Hour minus 1, the crock was brought up to the bar and much Bourbon was added, the contents stirred. Now, Dad was getting into the spirit: "Johnson, how many silver ladles have you dissolved in this formula?" "Don't rightly know, Mr. Acheson. Quite a few." Half an hour before guest time, the frosted silver mugs were brought out to the bar and packed with crushed ice. Sprigs of fresh mint were added and the chemically rich Bourbon formula, all but radioactive, was ladled into the mugs. Just enough time elapsed for melting ice to dilute the drinks an iota before the guests arrived. Dad's last admonition was part of the annual rite: "Johnson, go easy on second helpings or you'll have everyone on their ear." "I'll do that, Mr. Acheson. I'll just slow down the service." It was a strategy that came naturally.

Two hours later, the guests had gone. There was no need to linger over mint juleps. Dad was mellow. "Well done, Johnson. Those were the best mint juleps ever." "Yes sir. That's what you said last year."

Dad: "And it was true last year."

Johnson: "Maybe next year I'll make 'em better than this year."

The courtroom lawyer was still alert and alive, and the trap easily avoided. "Never, Johnson. Never."

Rolling Stock

T O MY FATHER, automobiles were both a necessity and a means of satisfying gadget fascination. He loved a new car, the smell of oil and leather, the novel configuration of the dashboard, the graceful styling, the ever greater power that successive models produced. He was particularly drawn to convertibles. In the 1920s through the mid-thirties, he especially liked the full sedan four-door model, with open sides and a full-length convertible top—the "touring car." One of the first of this genre in my memory was a Willys Overland, a rugged car, good for rough country roads and summer weather. It was housed, when in the country, in a shed without doors, protected from the weather but open to invasion by all manner of insects, mice, bats, and birds (the farm might well have been named "Bat City"). A colony of wasps built their characteristic gray paper nest in the corner of the roof of the Willys, effectively grounding the car for some time. This and bird droppings persuaded Dad to enclose the shed so as to make a proper garage; invasions thereafter were limited to mice, which were little inconvenienced by locked doors.

The Willys was function without much form. Black, rec-

tangular, and underpowered, it had no appeal to the Irish in
Dad's character, and it was soon accompanied by a Model A
Ford bought from the Cherner Motor Company, a Washington dealer, secondhand. Cherner's motto was: "Next to a new
car, a 'Chernerized' car is best." The Model A was high off the
ground. Even a juvenile passenger had a bird's-eye view of the
world. The engine, a small six-cylinder affair, was quiet and had
an audible beat rhythm, at about a sixteenth note, rather like
The African Queen. It had more pep than the Willys, and for a
time Dad was satisfied. It was a hardtop coupe, with roll-up
windows and a rumble seat. Dad let us children ride in the
rumble seat where we craned our heads out the side, the way
dogs feel the wind past their ears.

Shortly after the Model A, Dad lost his heart to a light blue
Chrysler touring car, long, graceful, fast, with sleek, fluid styling and chrome wings on the radiator cap. The year must have
been about 1930. With the canvas top down, and riding in the
rear seat, one felt like European royalty, and this car was a
favorite of all ages. It was a debonair car and fueled Dad's taste
for glamour.

In cold weather, as when we drove to the farm in winter for
brush clearing, touring cars required that one snap on the isin-
glass curtains to cover the open sides. Even so, cold air flowed
freely into the back seat. Heaters were unheard of. Children
complained, and Dad came home one day with the first model
of Ford's V-8 engine car, another "Chernerized" hardtop
coupe with a rumble seat. This only partially solved the cold
problem, for a freezing juvenile had to be shifted to the cabin,
while a comfortable juvenile was rotated from the cabin to the
freezing and uncommunicable world of the rumble seat. Dad

administered this justice fairly enough, for the standards of the time.

In this period of the early thirties the most elegant car of all entered our lives. It was a big car, a touring car, a graceful and stylish car, a Pierce Arrow. A dark, polished green, with exterior luggage trunk, elongated engine hood, metal spare tire cases set in the left and right front fenders, headlight nacelles rising in a gradual fluid line from the front of the fender, the Pierce Arrow was among the most elegant cars ever made in America. Dad's instinct for style had finally met its mate. Easily fourteen feet long, it steered like a truck and was underpowered for the great weight it had to propel. Dad grumbled about the Pierce Arrow's uphill performance—a five-degree grade required a shift of gears. But downhill the Pierce Arrow was hard to beat.

Dad was a responsible if zesty driver. He moved along, but obeyed the rules. The character of the car seemed to enter his personality when he drove, though he did not have much of an idea of engineering or of what went on under the hood. If a car began to give him trouble, he lost interest in it, as he might lose interest in a young law associate whose work disappointed him. When Johnson, the butler-chauffeur, entered our lives, Dad naturally delegated all auto maintenance matters to him. Dad's characteristic analysis of a balky car went like this: "Johnson, I had the Ford out today. The damn thing doesn't run right. Take it down to Cherner and see what the trouble is." Thereafter, Dad's romance with the offending car cooled quickly and inevitably moved to some other model, a triumph of hope over experience, as Samuel Johnson said of second marriages.

After the Pierce Arrow there were many other cars, each

reflecting some facet of Dad's personality. There was the Packard 120 (for dash), in which I came to grief in Murray Bay, Quebec. There was a 1932 Studebaker with a releasable clutch feature on the gear shift (for gadget fascination), a 1934 Ford V-8 convertible (for power), a 1941 wooden Ford station wagon (for the country squire role), a seven-passenger 1938 Buick limousine (for luxury), a 1941 Buick convertible (for dash, again), and in the postwar years another sky blue Chrysler convertible (return to first love). Of all Dad's cars, that was perhaps his favorite, and perhaps the best, a trustworthy friend. But I think when he drove it, he relived driving the Chrysler touring car with the wings on the radiator cap: he was thirty-six years old again, a debonair, dashing young man with the world before him.

Center Court

AROUND 1926 OR 1927 I first became aware that my parents played tennis. We were visiting Dad's parents in Middletown, Connecticut (his father by then was Episcopal Bishop of Connecticut). Mother and Dad left the house with tennis rackets to play on the Wesleyan University courts across the small park from my grandparents' house. This seemed to me an odd circumstance without an explanatory antecedent, something I had never seen them do.

A few years later (perhaps 1929–30) my parents began taking my older sister and me to the Manor Club not far from the farm and started us out on tennis—holding the racket, learning the bounce, attempting to hit the ball over the net. Dad was not a patient teacher, and most of this instruction fell to Mother. After a fair amount of drill we were allowed a lemonade and a swim in the pool. This basic instruction took hold; my sisters and I learned the rudiments and started to play each other. A few boys in and around Sandy Spring played; the Hyde and Farquhar families had clay courts.

Dad now fell into the grip of one of his fierce enthusiasms.

We must all become accomplished tennis players. We must build a tennis court, take lessons, and uphold the family honor in the community. The court was duly built, of red clay, some sixty yards to the west of the house. No trees provided any shade. The clay should have had more sand mixture to absorb water, but instead seemed all clay, either too wet and slippery to play, or baked to an adobe consistency like the ancient brick cities of Zimbabwe. It was a highly labor-intensive court, requiring several hours a week of watering and rolling. Periodic shipments of sand were trucked in to leaven the uncompromising red clay, but the sand blew off in the wind and washed off in the rain. Tennis balls immediately acquired a reddish hue; socks and tennis shoes became permanently impregnated with a red dust. Male children, of which I was the sole specimen, were assigned the labor. When the court was very dry, the clay became powdered under foot and blew away in the wind, eventually exposing the top of the gravel substratum.

Dad marshaled the troops. We were provided with rackets from Feron in New York, where Dad went regularly on legal business. He realized that most of his children had reached a capability for the game, modest as it was, that was the limit of his ability to teach, so he broke the news that we were to have a session twice a week with a teaching professional (the only kind, since professional purse tournaments did not exist at that time). On the appointed day, he arrived.

Otto Glockler, as his name was, had been the pro at a couple of prominent country clubs in the Washington area, and was at that time a freelance instructor. To be generous, I will call him 5 feet 6. He had a spry but unmistakably mature figure. He wore a white linen cap, white linen plus-four knickerbockers, and had the eye and reflexes of a cat. Otto approached his instruction task with admirable clarity. First learn the rhythm, bounce, and behavior of the ball. Then learn the basic forehand and backhand strokes. Both were to be hit with the eastern grip—the edge of the racket ran straight down the divide between thumb and forefinger. The stroke was to be two-dimensional on either backhand or forehand, i.e., in a plane parallel to the ground, without three-dimensional complexities like chop or top spin. This allowed a minimum of variables to go wrong with the stroke. The serve was to be a firm, but not strenuous, overhead stroke, not much back twist, not a high toss, a little bevel of the racket to send the ball off to the left of the receiver's court (assuming a right-handed server). This was meat-and-potatoes tennis. The instruction stretched over many weeks.

Otto taught the volley in a sound way that suited the construction of the human body. The forehand volley must be hit well away from the body with a pretty flat racket face and a slight under spin to finish the stroke. The backhand volley was to be hit close to the body with a straight-out punch and flat racket face.

Dad liked power in the shot, but had little time or patience for the study of spin, angle, or change of pace. The forehand volley, basically the most unnatural shot, eluded him permanently. He loved the backhand volley, and would come charging to the net after serve, eyes distended, ready for the fatal punch with his backhand, right off the belt buckle. His mustache turned particularly fierce in the second before the punch,

Center (and only) court at Harewood Farm: The author (*left*) and Dad (*right*),

like a Polish lancer about to administer the fatal thrust. His serve was firm, but not very hard; I doubt that he knew how to swing from the lower back.

Otto did his work well and departed. After that we were on our own. I was just beginning a lifetime addiction to the game and my sisters also were to become competent tennis players. Dad began recruiting us to play as his doubles partner in weekend matches and tournaments around Sandy Spring. From my perspective, this proved to be a mixed pleasure and trial. We were both temperamental and became irritated and frustrated by our errors, doubly so by the errors of the other partner. I served many double faults, trying for a strong offensive second serve. Dad was quick to counsel: "Just get the second serve in."

circa 1939–40.

This was such reasonable advice, and so obviously called for, that it always put me in a bad temper. When he overhit a forehand volley, as he was wont to do, I did not conceal disappointment. And so we tended to demoralize each other. Dad sometimes said to me before a match: "Now, don't get upset by your mistakes and act like Fred Perry on an off day." Since Fred Perry was very high on the equanimity scale, I always disregarded the advice and acted like someone else on an off day.

In 1938, my parents took all of us to France and England. Dad had heard about permanent tennis court lines, tapes made of lead, which one could buy in London at Jacques, a firm widely known for sporting equipment. The lines on the court at

the farm were initially of lime powder, laid down by a slotted
machine like a grass seeder. This system was superseded by
cloth tapes. These were a pain; they had to be stapled to the
earth at about twelve-inch intervals and quickly turned the
color of the Zimbabwe red clay. Dad had been put on to lead
tapes by his close friend, Colonel Raymond E. Lee, then the
military attaché at the U.S. Embassy in London. Lead tapes
were duly delivered to our London hotel. Consternation! The
set weighed perhaps 600 pounds and came in boxes that no one
could lift. They were ordered redelivered to our boat for the
return voyage and eventually found their way to the farm.

Dad's high-tech solution to the issue of the lines proved a
disappointment. The lead tapes came with holes every several
inches into which fitted nails were driven. The whole notion of
nailing something to red clay ignored the biblical parable of
"the house founded upon sand." Rain and wind soon eroded
the clay from the areas adjacent to the lines, leaving shallow
ridges of clay, each protected by a lead roof. These armored
ridges were ankle-turners of the most lethal kind. Soon the
white paint disappeared from the lead tapes, leaving the lines
invisible from the opposite side of the net. From time to time
the tapes were taken up, the red clay ridges leveled, the tapes
repainted, measured off, and laid down again. As I had the
laborious part in these processes, I was not impressed with
Britain's supposedly labor-free lines. Nevertheless, Dad retained his faith in the lead tapes and was proud of this unique
equipment which had become something of a conversation
piece around Sandy Spring. He told every visiting player:
"These tapes are a marvelous British invention. Permanent,
absolutely no trouble to maintain."

Designs and Crafts

T
HOUGH MARRIED TO AN ARTIST, Dad was far from "arty." He respected good art, by which he meant established art. He liked a few of the French Impressionists, chiefly Renoir and Monet. He liked Degas and Van Gogh, not so much Cézanne or Matisse. He did not like to spend time in galleries. So far as I know, he never tried his own hand with oils or watercolors, but admired and encouraged Mother's painting, which was very good, and let that speak to the world for the family.

In a way it was surprising that Dad did not paint, for he was a competent draftsman and had a good eye for color and detail. Early in our life at Harewood Farm he had a local builder make a shed by the kitchen for firewood (for some years the main cooking stove was wood-burning). Dad's drawing for the construction was a bit above the station of the structure itself, employing two Palladian arches on each side of the shed. Dad liked the Palladian form and enjoyed doing the concept drawings for new construction, aware that Thomas Jefferson worked in a similar way and was Palladio's most influential advocate in this country. Dad liked the idea of a skill and a style shared with

Dean Acheson in Alice Acheson's Harewood Farm Italianate studio, 1960s.
PHOTO © BY JILL KREMENTZ

Jefferson. He understood the pleasing quality of the curved shape. One of his designs was a white palisade front gate for the roadway entrance to our farm property, in which the gate curved up to the center from the two high white brick gateposts at the side, from which low white palisade wings curved away in crescents—very graceful.

Dad liked aesthetic approbation. When he had committed a design to paper, sooner or later it appeared during family idle time. Then it was: "What do you think of this?" and the drawing was dropped with a flourish on the table. This was not

136

The gate of Dad's design, attended by Alice and Mary Acheson, and Duffy.

understood as an open invitation to candid criticism. Alternative suggestions received a polite but cool response. The family was a cheering section, not a design committee.

By the late 1940s we children were all married, finished with the war, and living independently, visiting the farm occasionally. When Dad's first grandchild, a girl, was just a few years old, Dad hit on an idea to keep her occupied and absorbed while the rest of us were pursuing activities of no interest to her. The idea was a walk-in, reduced-scale playhouse. Out came the sheets of graph paper, soon covered with floor plans, elevations, details of plans. In a very few days the house was done, equipped with a window bench, chairs and tables to the scale of a three-to-four-year-old. On small shelves rested small plates, cups and saucers; miniature tea settings appeared on the

Eldie's playhouse at Harewood Farm and the master builder, 1950s.

table. Granddaughter and her doll friends had tea together while adults were otherwise occupied. A few years later Dad built to scale a portable dollhouse of two stories, with miniature furniture, which helped the same grandchild pass many a rainy day.

Perhaps like Jefferson, Dad was no advocate of simplicity in design. He wanted it to be expressive, and found no merit in Puritan self-restraint. The family flag comes to mind. In the 1950s, Dad was taken by the notion of a flagpole at the farm that would carry yardarms bearing the Maryland flag and a family flag that Dad would design himself. It was clear from

138

the start that this flag was to be a vehicle for artistic self-expression of a rare order. Soon the rest of us were permitted to gaze on the product of the master's labor, a full-size painted paper model, 3 x 4 feet.

The flag had five elements, each representing some facet of the family roots: a round center and four rectangular quarter sections. In the center was a red rooster standing on a trumpet; above, a small pennant bearing the word "VIGILANTIBUS." This

device, in fact our hereditary family seal, can be seen on the iron gates of Acheson House on the Royal Mile in Edinburgh to this day. In one quarter was the seal of Connecticut, the nutmeg vine, representing Dad's state of birth; in another the wolverine of Michigan, Mother's birth state. In the third quarter was the gold harp of Ireland on a green field (Mother's ancestry), and in the fourth quarter the red maple leaf of Canada (Dad's maternal ancestry). The flag was beautiful, eye-catching, and defensibly authentic. The yellow and black checkered flag of Maryland and the Acheson flag together were a dizzying sight, usually prompting the question from first-time visitors: "What on earth is that?"

A little before he became Secretary of State, Dad had a new workshop built to accommodate some power tools. This was greatly to facilitate do-it-yourself carpentry around the farm and was to launch Dad on many years of cabinetmaking. He had been looking for some basic power tools for working with wood: a heavy drill, a joiner, a lathe, a planer, and a bench saw, all to be bolted to the floor. Purchased new, these would have cost several thousand dollars, which was too rich for Dad's purse, so Dad went around to White's hardware store at Norbeck to see what might be available secondhand, and asked to be alerted if anything turned up. One day he got a call from White's: "Mr. Acheson, you know that retired admiral I told you about? Well he came in here this morning with one hand done up in bandages, and I think I can get a set of power tools for you, cheap!"

The power tools were duly installed, and Dad began to turn out a few simple pieces of furniture: a magazine rack, end tables, stools, benches. These were neat and sturdy, with

---

On the opposite page: Dean Acheson in his workshop at Harewood Farm, and the early-American style dining-room hutch produced in the workshop.
PHOTOS © BY JILL KREMENTZ

rounded or scalloped corners, and firmly jointed. Soon his aspirations grew. For me he made a bar of ¾-inch cherry, a bar to endure for the ages, with neat bronze hardware. For one of my sisters he built perhaps his most ambitious piece, a highboy carved to hold and show plates and silver. For me, again, a desk of plain early American design with a shallow center drawer allowing lots of legroom, four side drawers, and legs of graceful, tapered delicacy, turned on his lathe. Dad liked to do drawers because they were forgiving: "If you botch a drawer, you can turn it around and put the bad end on the inside," as he put it; for all I know, a thought shared by Chippendale.

Dad's workshop had a space-saving feature of his own invention. The overhead 2 by 4 beams which lent rigidity to the building were perhaps a foot over Dad's head. To the underside of those beams he nailed the lids of jars. The glass jar could then be screwed into the lid by reaching a few inches over his head. In these jars he kept all his assorted screws and nails, so that the contents could be ascertained simply by looking up. This saved horizontal bench space and shelf space, and made for a singularly uncluttered workshop.

When Dad became Secretary of State, it was a time of bitter partisanship in domestic politics and extreme tension in foreign affairs. He was under a lot of pressure from both sources. He believed, nevertheless, in doing the nation's business in the working week and getting away from it on the weekend, an attitude that came naturally to him and was strongly reinforced by General Marshall's example. Dad never lived the workaholic pattern that became a fashion in the Kennedy administration and has left a malign mark on all its successors. In this respect the farm was Dad's saving and cabinetmaking his escape. He learned that when one is loafing or reading or weeding the garden, the mind tends to return to the worries that were preoccupying it, but when one is turning a table leg on a lathe or running a corner board through a joiner, concentration must be total, to the exclusion of everything else. Thus loafing is not relaxing; concentration is. Escape is complete. It was during this trying time in his life that Dad turned out a great profusion of furniture for friends and family, making good his periodic escape from tension and keeping his sense of proportion and sanity.

Dad's family never forgot the admiral with the bandaged fingers. We were always after Dad to adopt rigid precautions to keep his fingers away from cutting edges. He complied and made a twelve-inch notched stick with which he pushed the boards through the power saw, planer, and joiner. This stick took several hits early on and Dad got religion quickly and thoroughly.

In the 1950s, Dad commenced a whirlwind romance, lasting to a durable affair, with flowers. Someone gave him a few bulbs of gladiolus and they were planted in Mother's flower garden at the farm. The result was intoxicating to Dad, so the next spring several rows of the old vegetable garden were plowed up and gladioli of many varieties were planted—nearly sixty to seventy yards of gladioli. It became his new enthusiasm, following the familiar steep, linear curve of earlier enthusiasms. The whole lower garden blazed with gladioli—salmon pink, scarlet, magenta, so deep a purple as to be nearly black, white, all by the tens of yards. When in bloom, they filled the house, were given to friends by the basketful, an entire car seatful taken to Dad's office periodically. In the fall, Dad took up the

Alice and Dean Acheson in their garden at Harewood Farm. ACME PHOTO

bulbs and put them in buckets with mothballs for storage over the winter. The mothballs seemingly killed any parasites that might be lurking in the bulbs, for in the following year, when replanted, the bulbs burst forth with even more vigor and profusion.

With Dad, one never knew what would happen when a current fad reached a fatal incandescence. In this case a frequent pattern—boom and bust—was not followed. Dad cut back on gladioli, but took a lateral turn into a different mode. This was to be a garden rivaling Mother's varied and beautifully kept garden, but with a unique theme: a white garden. Anything white qualified. Thirty yards or so of tall and short flowers were planted in a bed perhaps six feet wide, separated from Mother's garden by a grape arbor—a decent separation, lest invidious comparisons be drawn. Hollyhocks, snapdragons, gladioli, lilies, impatiens, daisies, Queen Anne's lace all were massed into a garden that was a moonlike monochrome world, the eye taken by surprise and the brain left wondering where the color went. White became for Dad what black had been for Henry Ford I—the only color. Dad's big moment came when luncheon guests arrived, as was common on a Sunday, and Dad escorted them to the white garden. "What do you think of that?"

Icing the President

I T WAS A LAZY, HOT Sunday morning in early summer in 1951 (give or take a year). My wife and I were booked to go to the farm for lunch and were reading the paper at home in Washington. Then the telephone; it was Dad for me. "Dave, President Truman is coming for lunch today, and we don't have enough ice. Will you get some block ice on your way here and come a little early?"

Serious ice requirements at the farm were met with ice in thirty-pound blocks, kept in an old-fashioned ice chest outside the kitchen. Sunday lunch in summer always posed serious ice requirements: ice for cocktails; ice for iced tea; ice for water glasses; and ice for the hand-cranked ice cream maker— crushed ice with rock salt in the cooling jacket for effective chilling. There was a general store at Sandy Spring with a block ice vendor, our usual source of supply.

Soon my wife and I were under way, allowing for a thirty-minute margin. Stopping at the Sandy Spring store, we were horrified to find the ice sold out. It was a hot season and the run on ice had depleted it by Saturday evening. Shaken by this reverse, we backtracked to Olney, two miles west, where there was a general store with an ice vendor at the main intersection. Again, sold out! We were now running out of time, but shot off toward Brookville, to the north. Finally, there was a gas station along the road and outside it a vending unit with a sign: "BLOCK ICE." In double time we bought ninety pounds of ice and sped off to the farm, hoping to arrive before the President. Minutes after the ice was unloaded, the presidential limousine (and security escort) swept through the white, curved palisade gate of Dad's own design and out stepped the guest of honor.

President Truman was dressed in flawless summer casual fashion: starting at the top, he sported a white linen golf cap—not the baseball cap model, but the 1930s Palm Beach model. Next came a tropical print sport shirt, short-sleeved and open at the neck. Then sand-colored linen slacks, pleated, with matching socks. Finally, he was shod in white and brown wing-tip shoes, perfectly cleaned and polished. This was all classic Gold Coast resort dress—one missed only the palm trees and Rudy Vallee in the background.

The President was the soul of cordiality. We learned that Mrs. Truman and Margaret were taking a holiday in Independence and that, with the Korean War going full blast, the President felt he should stay close to Washington. "That place [meaning the White House] is mighty lonely on a weekend. You nice people have saved my life."

Dad took charge of the program. Would the President care to swim? He would. Soon we were all changed to bathing suits and walking across the field to the pool at the edge of the woods. The President's bathing suit revealed a stocky, strong figure, clearly durable and vigorous. Dad gave him the two-minute briefing on the Quaker community of Sandy Spring, the eighteenth-century farm, the ice water in which we were to experience immersion. President Truman listened attentively.

The security detail had seemingly disappeared, but as we neared the pool my wife noted, *sotto voce,* that every rhododendron and mountain laurel seemed to be wearing a fedora hat. The detail was, in fact, barely seen and totally unheard.

The President "came to swim," as the sportswriters say, and immediately put down his towel and glasses and plunged in. His considerable displacement kicked up a small tidal wave, as Dad advanced more cautiously from the shallow end and pushed off into deep water. The President exclaimed at the frigid water and named a few newspaper writers he would like to throw in. In a few minutes the conversation, largely commanded by the President, engaged matters of leadership during a war, the difficulties experienced by Mr. Lincoln during his war, the tendency of politicians—and people generally—to avoid hard choices, the burden on Generals Grant and Sherman to show a turnaround in their war by the election campaign of 1864. The President spoke easily about American history, in clear and plain terms, and was obviously comfortable in facing what he had to do.

As we swam, the echoes of spaced shotgun fire reached us from beyond the woods. This produced quite a stir among the fedoras until Dad explained that this was a rural community and a neighboring farmer sometimes practiced on clay pigeons on the weekend.

Thoroughly chilled, we returned to our respective quarters, dressed, and gathered on a brick patio behind the house. The unruffled Johnson approached bearing a tray with a large cocktail shaker and glasses. This signaled the arrival of the Harewood Special, a genial drink of ½ lime juice, ¼ white rum, ¼ gin, a dash of Grenadine (for color), and chopped mint, shaken or blended with very little sugar and plenty of ice. A whispered question to Johnson evoked the assurance that the ice supply looked good—but then, we were only starting to use it.

Throughout cocktails, Mr. Truman maintained a cheerful, candid, gracious, amusing demeanor, becoming more convivial as the Harewood Specials were circulated and found their way to the presidential metabolism.

During lunch, the conversation turned to the disastrous deterioration (dry rot) and ongoing restoration of the White House structure (a second-story floor had partially collapsed and the Trumans were living at Blair House across the street). The iced tea and water glasses were repeatedly filled. I looked at the inscrutable Johnson for reassurance that we had a comfortable balance in the ice account, but no readable sign came back. Then came the hand-cranked ice cream, which made a big hit with Mr. Truman.

Finally, the meal over, we trooped out on the lawn to a stand of lawn furniture, which included some ancient steamship folding canvas chairs. The President made a beeline for one of those. "After that wonderful lunch, I'm just going to let myself back in one of those steamer chairs," he said. As he lowered his solid frame into the tilt-back chair, there was a brief, low noise like the tearing of cloth—indeed, it *was* the tearing of cloth. Down went the President, through the canvas, the seat of his sand-colored linen slacks firmly on the grass, his head raised in surprise between the wooden arms of the steamer chair. A second of horrified silence was broken by the President's laugh. "Well, Mrs. Acheson, they never fed me well enough at the White House to put me through the furniture!" Much relieved laughter on all sides. Coffee was brought. Mr. Truman had become a member of the family. More good talk ensued.

With obvious reluctance, Mr. Truman rose as the time neared four o'clock. "I've got to get back before someone finds out I'm not essential. Thanks for a wonderful day." Without long goodbyes, he went to his car, and he and his security retinue drove out through the gate.

Johnson approached with a tray to pick up the coffee cups, as Dad breathed a deep sigh of relief. "Johnson," he said, "we're lucky we didn't run out of ice." "We just did," said Johnson. "The President and the ice left in a dead heat."

De Gustibus

"OF MATTERS OF TASTE there can be no dispute," or in
the old Latin saying, "De gustibus non disputan-
dum est." But tastes, taken together, say much
about personality.

What were Dad's tastes? What did they say about him?
We can take some small things first and move on to larger ones.

Dad was widely known for his taste in clothes, which was
discussed fully in an earlier chapter. For someone as fastidious
as Dad in matters of dress, he was surprisingly simple in matters of food and drink. No tragedy that he did not live into the
age of *nouvelle cuisine.* Fussy little portions of artistically dis-
played food would have irritated him, as certain modern art
did, evoking, "Who do they think they're kidding?" Dad was
basically a protein man: roast of lamb, beef, or pork, sausage,
bacon, scrambled eggs, chicken, chops were his regular favorites. The vegetable kingdom he regarded with a discriminating
skepticism, believing that man's ingenuity and versatility in
vegetable culture far outstripped the merits of the material.
Corn on the cob, lima beans, succotash, string beans, cold as-
paragus, mashed and baked potatoes, fresh garden peas, and

broiled tomatoes all stood at the head of the class. In the tolerable zone were cooked carrots, steamed or boiled beets, and summer squash. Turnips, other forms of squash, zucchini, and most other vegetable forms he regarded as unwelcome occupants of valuable space on the table and in the garden. His mother's recipe for succotash, done with a little salt pork rendered into the corn and lima beans, with lots of black pepper, was perhaps his all-time favorite dish and was served frequently.

Seafood and Dad were made for each other. A running dilemma with him was whether raw clams or oysters were the tastier dish. Sometimes he took a half dozen of each, only to pronounce the contest a draw. Lobster in the shell and crab Maryland were special favorites. He loved fried fish, particularly fresh water fish (perch, trout, bass) for breakfast, lunch, or dinner. Desserts, except fruit, left Dad pretty cold. He liked hot soup and cold soup, particularly oxtail, pepper pot, and Vichyssoise.

Parallel, in a way, to Dad's taste in food—good, but not fancy—ran his taste in drink. Carbonated drinks made him hiccup, which allowed only an occasional beer, ginger ale, scotch and soda, or champagne. In the 1930s it seems to me that his favorite cocktail was an old-fashioned, but by the time he ended his service in the State Department the dry Martini had swept the competition from the field. Martinis often reminded him of F.D.R. serving Martinis in the Oval Office. These F.D.R. shook up himself in a large silver shaker, holding his thumb over the spout to substitute for the missing stopper. There were exceptions to the supremacy of the Martini. For a Sunday lunch cocktail at the farm in the summer there was the

De Gustibus

Harewood Special, a kind of sugarless Daiquiri with a little gin and chopped mint added. The Special went down the hatch as painlessly as yogurt and administered a sly rabbit punch half an hour later. The other exception was also seasonal, when Mother and Dad took their annual vacation in Antigua. There they and their friends went native, wore shorts and sandals, played croquet, and drank a rum-and-lime sour with nutmeg grated over the top.

Dad thought champagne was a woman's drink, though he would take a champagne cocktail if nothing else were available. His taste in red and white table wine was discriminating, but far from sophisticated. His wine dealer, he said, had forgotten more than Dad would ever know—why not rely on him?

From the time Dad majored in English literature at Yale he was an avid reader, with a taste for rich, boisterous fiction classics and biography. Smollett and Dickens attracted him for their vivid, sharp characters and the vitality of the action. He liked to read history of desperate, challenging experiences—the Peloponnesian War, the American Civil War—which tested people to the limit. He read a lot of biography, much of it about nineteenth-century British statesmen, again preferring characters of originality and dash, like Disraeli, rather than Gladstone and some of the social reformers, whom he dismissed as "Christers." In the 1920s and '30s he read a fair share of current literature about American society and public policy, with much sympathy for the underdog, the workingman.

It never failed to surprise people who knew him in later life that, freshly out of law school, Dad had written a book on the need for a new labor jurisprudence. Its thesis was that owners of a factory did not have the right to exact from their workers

unreasonable terms of employment based merely upon owner-
ship of the factory, but that duties of mutual support and a
more bilateral social bargain were inherent in the industrial
capital-labor relationship. To support this thesis, he drew upon
the common law of feudal times in England. The lord owned
the land and the serf had to work and fight for the lord, but the
law also enforced the lord's obligation to house and feed the
serf, to defend him from danger, to respond to his need for
adjudication, to answer his grievances, etc. This, Dad believed,
was a fair bargain from which the industrial society had retro-
gressed. The book was offered to the Harvard Law School for
publication, but never appeared in print. In any case, Dad was
still "liberal" in his views about domestic society well into his
middle age, until he felt that violence, crime, and disorder had
gotten entirely out of control. His library reflected a liberal cast
of mind. When, in his advancing age, he was often kidded
about his intellectual migration "from Brandeis to Bismarck"
(as the taunt was put), he defended himself vigorously on the
strength of his early pro-labor credentials and his continuing
loyalty to the Democratic Party's domestic agenda.

Dad died in 1971. The last presidential candidate for whom
he voted, therefore, was the 1968 candidate, Hubert Hum-
phrey, an old friend. People have sometimes asked me if the
1972 Democratic Convention and the McGovern campaign
would have pushed Dad over to Nixon, had Dad lived another
year. This is an unprofitable speculation. He would have been
distressed at the evolution of the Democrats, and by 1971 he
had come to find some constructive qualities in President
Nixon. More could not be said with any assurance. A clue
available in Dad's papers comes from a letter written in 1970

Dean Acheson at his desk in the guest house of Harewood Farm, 1971.
PHOTO: © JILL KREMENTZ

155

just after the congressional elections: ". . . My own party is disorganized, bankrupt and without first-class leadership."*

Dad's sense of humor owed much to two quite different streams of influence. From his father and his Ulster ancestry came a lively sense of the ridiculous, a gift of mimicry, a talent for droll stories. He really got into a role, using eyes, eyebrows, bass or treble voice, and extravagant manual gestures. Making people laugh gave him great pleasure, and what political Washington might judge to be limits imposed by discretion meant absolutely nothing to him. He often said, in different ways: "I'm not a candidate for office and I won't live like a nervous, stuffed shirt lawyer." Another stream of influence was his own outlook on life, hopeful but realistic and sardonic, reinforced by his admiration for Justice Holmes and Holmes's similar style. Dad liked an ironic edge to his, and other people's stories. One of his favorites was his own father's story of overtaking a man walking in the same direction, as Bishop Acheson (then a church rector) was walking home for dinner from his rectory in Middletown. As the churchman came near, he heard the man mumbling; as he passed, the words became clear: "When I get home, if dinner isn't ready I'm going to raise hell; if it is ready, I won't eat a God-damned bite!" Another favorite was Konrad Adenauer's comment to him: "How improvident of the Almighty to limit man's intelligence without limiting his stupidity." Close to his all-time favorite was a brief exchange with Count Sforza, then Foreign Minister of Italy, at a NATO Council meeting. A messenger wearing a somber expression entered the meeting room and handed the Count a note. Dad

*Letter to Sir Roy Welensky, Nov. 16, 1970, *Among Friends*, p. 318.

was sitting next to him. The Count read the brief note, and leaned over to whisper confidentially to Dad, "My government has fallen." Dad immediately thought of disruption to the long-range agenda and whispered back: "My goodness, that could be very serious." The last whisper was the Count's: "No, desperate, perhaps, but not serious." Dad's comment when he reported this sidebar was: "No wonder the Italians are able to rise above their problems."

Social life was both a bane and a joy to Dad. In the 1920s and 1930s he and Mother were much sought after by Washington society and by embassies. They were a bright, attractive, and spirited couple, full of irreverence for Washington norms. George Rublee, one of Dad's senior partners, described Dad as "the shiniest fish that ever came out of the sea." Their friends ranged from the Olympian George Rublee to Sinclair ("Red") Lewis, the novelist, and his hard-drinking set. Mother and Dad found Washington society dull and complacent, but accepted and returned invitations as a matter of courtesy. It was in character for Dad to say at an embassy party during National Prohibition: "Well, I'm not running for office and I *do* want a drink." This side of social life was a bane. The joy was evenings with their bright and irreverent friends, talking about letters, history, politics, social policy. Dad liked lively people, novel ideas, intellectual stimulus and shock. He loved laughter, clever argument, outrageous humor. He liked things to come together neatly, with a click, with no intellectual parts left over and none missing. He hated cant and hypocrisy, particularly when it was for show. He hated the pompous, the obvious, the pedantic.

Dad got a kick out of representing the International Ladies'

Garment Workers' Union in the 1930s in an injunction suit in Kansas City (Mo.). It did not go over well at Covington, Burling, Rublee, Acheson & Shorb, who had major corporate clients, but Dad went ahead with it. He found David Dubinsky, president of the ILGWU, to be an authentic American original type: a Russian Jewish immigrant, smart, tough, dictatorial,

Dean Acheson with Ernest Bevin at the Foreign Office in London, 1950.
SPORT & GENERAL PHOTO

with a powerful belief in social justice to be achieved by industrial unionism, a character who might have stepped from Galsworthy's play, *Strife*. Dad found much the same satisfaction in rugged old Ernest Bevin, U.K. Foreign Secretary in the Attlee government and formerly head of the British dock workers' union. Once Bevin suborned Dad to sing with him "The Red Flag," the Labour Party anthem, which Dad found entertaining to do. While Dad disagreed with many Labour domestic policies, Bevin was his partner in foreign affairs. Moreover, Dad enjoyed stirring up the animals.

At a London conference where Dad and Bevin were representing their respective governments, Dad was invited to dine at the Bevins' flat, a home-cooked meal to be prepared by Mrs. Bevin. On Dad's arrival at the flat, Bevin took charge of cocktails. "I hear you like a dry Martini cocktail, Mr. Secretary, and I have learned the recipe." Duly, an ice-cold cocktail glass emerged from the pantry on a tray borne by Bevin. "Three to one, Mr. Secretary, just as they do in America." Dad eyed the yellowish mixture with trepidation, and took an exploratory sip. It was three to one, all right—three vermouth to one gin, in fact the original recipe invented by Martini & Rossi to promote sales of vermouth. Dad fought to keep his facial muscles under control and pronounced the drink excellent. At that point the telephone rang and Mrs. Bevin called her husband to answer it in the library, she being in the kitchen. Alone for a few moments, Dad found an innocent, helpless potted plant, and bestowed the Martini on the thirsty earth. Bevin returned in a few minutes. "Well, I see you finished your drink, let me make another." Dad responded: "That's nice of you, but I would like to see if I can equal your touch. That was a unique concoction," and off he went to the pantry.*

When Dad discovered a refreshing, unexpected streak in someone he thought he had typed, he was delighted, and a seed of affection was planted at that instant. In autumn of 1952, a year and a half after the political firestorm over President Truman's dismissal of General MacArthur as Commander in Chief in the Far East, Dad had to go to New York to attend and address the U.N. General Assembly. He and Mother stayed at the Secretary of State's suite in the Waldorf-Astoria Hotel, also General MacArthur's residence. Dad had no doubt of the correct thing to do: invite the MacArthurs to cocktails and make the *beau geste* to an erstwhile adversary (for Dad, with Averell Harriman, and Generals Marshall and Bradley, had advised the President to relieve MacArthur). To Dad's surprise, the MacArthurs accepted, and the two couples had an hour's animated conversation over Martinis, largely about Japan. Dad asked the general, then chairman of a major U.S. corporation, how he found big business and big businessmen, after a lifetime of public service. MacArthur's reply took Dad wholly by surprise and delighted him: "Acheson, I don't want to talk about those midgets!"

Like many of his generation, Dad's tastes in travel changed radically during his life. By today's standards he was not widely traveled until he became Secretary of State. He had no language facility. He visited Japan twice; once in the summer of 1915 when he and some Yale classmates were staked to the trip

*This is Dad's contemporaneous and oral report of this episode. It differs from that in the note to p. 387, *Present at the Creation.*

as a graduation present (by his mother); not again until 1962. His early travels with his parents were confined to Canada, western Europe, and England. During half his life, overseas travel had to be by boat. Jet travel did not become commonly available until Dad was nearly sixty-five years old. His generation was raised to be Anglophile, to regard northern and western Europe as civilized, and to study European languages and cathedrals.

In 1919 he visited the Hague, and in 1930 Stockholm on legal business. A good tale emanated from the second visit. The client was the Crown of Sweden, from which the United States had seized ships in U.S. ports during World War I. The purpose of the trip was to organize the facts underlying the claim of Sweden. Old King Gustav was king, a famous, tennis-playing monarch, then in his eighties. His habit was to stand at the net, on the center line, and volley anything within reach, leaving all else to his spry, younger doubles partner. During the lawyers' courtesy call at the royal palace, King Gustav inquired if any of the visiting legal team would like a tennis match. Dad was volunteered by his law partner and claimed by the king as his ally in doubles the following day. Two good players stood opposite. Deferring to protocol, Dad inquired: "Your majesty, do you prefer the backhand or forehand side?" The king replied: "Mr. Acheson, I will play the front court, you will play the back court." On this novel basis the match got under way, the king never moving from center net, Dad chasing all the lobs and passing shots on either side, corner to corner. By the end of the first set, the king was fresh and eager. "That was fun. Let's play another." Dad was red in the face and puffing. "I would love to, your majesty. Might we have a ten-minute rest?" "I'm surprised you need a rest, Mr. Acheson. I don't, and you are much younger." Dad realized the conversation had nowhere to go and let it drop. He always said he was lucky to live through this and should have charged double his hourly rates.

Jet travel opened up vistas in Dad's autumn of life that his spring and summer had never experienced. It became possible for him to travel in a day to England to take up a visiting lecturer position at Cambridge or receive an honorary degree at Oxford, to travel in a day to leisurely vacations in Antigua, to travel in a day to Italy, where he became enchanted by the country, the people, the food, the language, the high-speed life. Dad discovered fairly late in life that cold weather, hard currency, and dour northern respectability were not the sum of civilization. He became more hedonistic in his approach to travel and shed the long Anglophilia that came from his British father and Canadian mother. He wrote some short stories in which the ebullient Italian character was the hero, among them *The Big Fish of Como* in which a whopper is netted by umbrella.

Dad visited South America only once and in an official capacity, China only briefly in 1915, Russia never, Southeast Asia only once—in the 1960s as a lawyer for Cambodia. This paucity of travel to much of the world did not imply a lack of interest or curiosity, but priorities. In travel for pleasure, Dad wanted to have fun; he had little interest in cultural uplift. In official travel, Dad wanted to concentrate on the Eurocentric issues that he saw as the key to long-term political stability. There was not time to do everything.

In the summer of 1938 our family spent a considerable time in France, ending with a number of days in Paris where we stayed at the Elysée Parc Hotel. Dad learned that Endicott Peabody, the ancient Rector of Groton School, where I was a year away from graduation, was in town, and invited him and Mrs. Peabody to our suite for a drink and lunch. The Rector, who had ruled over Groton when Dad was there and still did, was now in his eighties, and a figure of awesome integrity and authority. Mrs. Peabody was sensitive, gracious, sweet, and petite. The audacity of Dad's invitation horrified me, not less because I knew of Peabody's abortive attempt to have Dad's parents withdraw him from the school. Said I: "You invited the Peabodys to have drinks?" "Why not?" was the response.

At the appointed hour the Peabodys arrived, he wearing a linen suit and a straw boater, the costume of a boulevardier. Disturbing reflections crowded into my mind. Had I misjudged this man? Had I oversimplified him? Was it possible that Dad knew what he was doing? The greetings were cordial. "Hello, Dean. I hope you and your family are enjoying Paris." "Hello, Mr. Peabody, Mrs. Peabody. How nice of you to come. We are having a fine time, thank you."

After a few minutes of chat, "Let me make you a drink." The Rector opted for gin and tonic, as did my parents. Mrs. Peabody chose sherry. Then the finger of fate pointed at me. "Anything to drink, Dave?" Since drinking at the school was categorically an expulsion offense, what degree of opprobrium attached to drinking before the Jove and Juno of my academic world? Before these charged particles of thought stopped crashing into each other, Mrs. Peabody spoke. "Do have something, David. We're all on holiday." This was an unmistakable passport, and I chose a French beer.

The conversation turned on the Czech Sudeten crisis, the

rotten state of French political morale, the passivity of France before Hitler, and the question what England would do. The Rector expressed confidence in Mr. Chamberlain, the Prime Minister. Dad expressed concern that Chamberlain underestimated Hitler's aims and opined that a tougher figure, perhaps Winston Churchill, was needed at 10 Downing Street. The Rector, who knew Chamberlain, expressed doubts about Churchill's stability—perhaps he wasn't quite a gentleman, as some of the Rector's British friends believed. These themes carried us through lunch.

When the Peabodys had gone, Dad said: "There goes a really great man, but do you know, there is a sad anomaly here. Chamberlain doesn't understand what he's up against, but he would be a great success as a student at Groton. Churchill does understand it. He would be kicked out of Groton in a week."

"Selective" would be an accurate term to describe Dad's cultural tastes and attainments. Avid a reader as he was and broadly knowledgeable about English literature, he was monolingual and thus had no access to a larger world of letters, except through translation. His taste in paintings and sculpture was straightforward and informed by a discriminating eye, but unsophisticated. He had not grown up with painters in the family; his interest in art, such as it was, derived from his marriage. Certain classical music he found pleasing—Handel, Brahms, Grieg—but he had little patience for sitting through symphonies or live musical recitals. When he *had* to go, as to Mrs. Robert Woods Bliss's musicales, it was out of social duty, not interest in the program. Interestingly, he enjoyed movies in rather a wide range of taste: the Tarzan films, *The Thin Man*, and the blood and thunder genre such as *The Prisoner of*

Zenda. Introspective films of mood and suffering, a familiar Swedish theme, bored him intensely. Certain musical comedies appealed to him—*South Pacific, My Fair Lady*—and those by his old friend, Cole Porter, but he required crispness, style, pace, and melody of a high order, or he started looking for the exit.

Dad was notorious for his distrust of the theatre, for too often the performance failed to live up to the billing. When the action bogged down, Dad was out the door, to the dismay of Mother and other theatre companions. When I was released from the Navy in the late autumn of 1945, prior to starting law school I stayed with my parents for a few weeks (my wife was in her last year at Bryn Mawr College). One night Mother had tickets to the National Theatre, so she, Dad, and I went to see Alfred Lunt and Lynne Fontanne perform. Near the end of the first act, Dad whispered in my ear: "I am leaving, ostensibly to go to the bathroom, but in reality to go home." Then he vanished. Mother was determined not to let his abscondment spoil our evening, so we stayed through. When Mother and I returned home, Dad was not there. Mother recalled that she had taken the house key from the hall tray. The other one was on the auto key ring, so Dad had been locked out. In about an hour the doorbell rang, and there was Dad, cheerful and unrepentant. "I had no key," he said, "so I went over to the Frankfurters and had a highball and a good talk with Felix." So much for Lunt and Fontanne.

This unwillingness to endure a passive imprisonment naturally made Dad a poor patient when illness struck. If he had to lie in bed at home with a flu, or a frequently rebellious stomach, he became testy, and the curve of testiness steepened sharply with time. Books, radio, work all failed to keep his mind off the irritating injustice he had to endure for the sake of some silly germ. He began to take liberties with the doctor's orders, to pad about the house, to telephone his friends at their offices.

On one occasion Dad was really ill, from a slight stroke, about eighteen months before his death. After a couple of weeks in the hospital he had recovered, seemingly, from all effects, or felt he had. Telephone conversations with him elicited the familiar symptoms of *ennui patientis.* The boredom increased, the irritation mounted. A jail break seemed imminent. He chafed particularly over the severe diet that his doctor thought warranted by his vascular condition. At this time it was my practice to stop and see him on my way home from work. One day my telephone rang: "Dave, are you planning to come by this afternoon?" Yes, I was. "Good. Would you stop by the Metropolitan Club and have them make up an order of the crab ravigotte and bring it over here? I can't stand any more of these damn vegetables!" The crab ravigotte was a truly Epicurean feast: crabmeat in a mustard-mayonnaise sauce, with slices of avocado; over the top a generous sprinkling of capers crowned with a liberal distribution of chopped hard-boiled egg. The club made up the order on a cardboard tray with plastic wrap firmly anchored over the assemblage.

As I approached Dad's hospital room, a nurse said: "Where are you going with that?" "It's for Mr. Acheson—he asked for it." "But he's on a strict diet." "Well," said I, "do you think he would ask for it if he didn't have his doctor's okay?" Happily, this question was allowed to pass, for the truthful answer would have been: "Of course!"

Felix Frankfurter

A S A PROFESSOR at the Harvard Law School after World War I, Felix Frankfurter—or "F.F.," as he was referred to by dozens of his students, law clerks, friends, and faculty colleagues—exerted a profound influence on Dad's early life. He was a stimulating teacher, who encouraged intellectual probes in directions that his students otherwise would probably not have undertaken. It was he, chiefly, who recruited Dad to come to Washington as law clerk—or "secretary" in the contemporary parlance—to Associate Justice Louis D. Brandeis, from which grew Dad's admiration of Brandeis and Holmes and his acquaintance and long partnership with Edward B. Burling. It was F.F. who encouraged Dad to write his book (mentioned earlier), soon after graduation, about the need for a new labor relations jurisprudence, and it was F.F. who brought Dad to President Roosevelt's attention in 1933.

It is possible that Dad might never have won his law degree at Harvard, but for the intervention of a Yale friend, Cole Porter, the famed writer of incomparable songs and musical comedies. Porter, the talented son of a wealthy Indiana manufacturer, was interested in popular composition while at Yale.

His father, hoping that he would take up a respectable business career, prevailed on young Porter to attend the Harvard Law School, where he, Dad, and a third man, now forgotten, rented a house as bachelors in Cambridge. Near mid-year Porter had completed a musical comedy which he financed and staged in Boston. On opening night the trio, the cast, and numerous friends stayed up until the newspaper reviews appeared in the wee hours. The show was unanimously deemed a brilliant success. Porter's claque then adjourned to the Cambridge house with champagne and put on a celebration that soon had the neighborhood agog.

The next morning complaints poured into the office of the Dean, the redoubtable Roscoe Pound, a Nebraska "dry." Pound, according to Dad's account, summoned the three housemates and told them that suspension seemed appropriate. Porter seized upon the silver lining in this cloud and asked for a private word with Pound. It was all his, Porter's, fault, he said. The other two, serious in their pursuit of the law, were misled from the true path by friendship and a sense of comradely support. Justice, said Porter, would be well served if he were expelled and the other two let off with an admonition. To Pound, this seemed fair, and the punitive example just as compelling as three suspensions. The deal was struck. Porter gained his freedom and went on to New York and musical Valhalla. Dad and the other housemate duly took their degrees.

But I digress. We return to Felix Frankfurter. F.F. was a small, tight package of energy, movement, and talk. He radiated mental and nervous power, and gave the impression that within his small stature productive faculties had been released and multiplied rather like nuclear fission. He would leap out of

Dean Acheson and Felix Frankfurter at the Senate Judiciary Committee hearings on the latter's appointment to the Supreme Court.

a chair and fly about the room in recounting a story, then—in emphasis—he would hold one by the arm in a grip of iron as he approached his point. His laugh was sharp, explosive. When he was in the room, he was naturally the magnet of attention.

Felix—as all of our family came to know him—came to Washington in 1939 when President Roosevelt appointed him to the Supreme Court of the United States. His confirmation by the Senate promised from the beginning to be controversial, and F.F. asked Dad to be his counsel during Senate Judiciary Committee hearings. This was a rebonding of their already close friendship that was to last another twenty-five years. At the hearings, Senator Pat McCarran of Nevada sought to expose Felix as a Communist sympathizer, on the strength of an alleged radical infection of the Harvard law faculty by Harold Laski, who had been visiting professor there during part of Frankfurter's tenure. The hearing was an unedifying affair in which McCarran read bits from Laski's writings and sought to have Frankfurter confirm that they carried a Communist message—which, of course, Frankfurter could not and would not do.

As Dad has written in his own memoirs, the end of the hearing was followed by client and lawyer celebrating with Senator Henry Ashurst (chairman of the full Judiciary Committee) in his office over a bottle of brandy, then moving the party to the White House, where they regaled President Roosevelt with war stories of the hearings and with Frankfurter's nuggets from American history revolving about the ill-fated romance of Catherine Chase and Senator Roscoe Conkling of New York in an earlier era. Dad always suspected that his future career in government was made that day, but a more formal president might have thought he had better ways to spend the time.

From that time on, Dad and Felix saw a great deal of each other. Both were widely read, both were something of Anglophiles, both loved current political gossip. Both believed in, and had known, Justice Holmes and adhered to the school of Holmes's credo of judicial self-restraint.

Soon after Felix's move to Washington, Dad and Felix began walking to work together. The drill was only slightly variable: sometimes Felix walked to our house and the two walked together to 15th and H streets, N.W., where the offices of Covington & Burling were situated. They were trailed by Felix's Supreme Court messenger in his own car (Felix neither drove nor owned a car). He then drove Felix from 15th & H to

Walking to work with Justice Felix Frankfurter. WIDE WORLD PHOTOS the Supreme Court. Sometimes Dad walked to the Frankfurter house and the dual walk went on from there. On a rainy day the messenger drove them to both destinations.

To say that these walks had an eclectic agenda would state it modestly. Felix regularly read several British newspapers, which often provided the conversational starting point. Felix believed that most social problems in the United States should be analyzed in the manner of a royal commission, like the Sankey Commission,* before legislative remedies were proposed. Dad was more skeptical about transplanting British parliamentary institutions. Often in their walks, Felix became so carried away that he stepped out in front of Dad and walked backward along the sidewalk while confronting his companion with full eye contact. These conversations caught the attention of passers-by and sometimes of reporters, and before long the town became acquainted with the animated nature of these walking dialogues as well as with the "Mutt and Jeff" dimensions of the principals.

Prior to 1941, the Frankfurter-Acheson route was usually (from Georgetown) south to Pennsylvania Avenue, then east to 15th Street. After Dad moved to the old State Department in the War-State-Navy Building at 17th Street and Pennsylvania Avenue, the route remained the same but was two blocks shorter. When the State Department moved to its present site, the route followed either Pennsylvania Avenue to 21st, then south to Virginia Avenue, or straight to Virginia Avenue from Georgetown and east to 21st.

---

*John (later Viscount) Sankey was chairman of the royal commission on the coal industry in 1919.

In 1947–48, a rare discord emerged to trouble these walks. The dedicated Zionists had succeeded in moving to the front burner of the U.S. agenda the issue of a new and separate Jewish state to be formed from British Palestine. The American Jewish community had made this an imperative that no American politician could ignore. Dad, out of office during much of this period, was opposed to such a state and against recognition of it by the government of the United States. He based this view on the certainty of volcanic Arab hostility and the prospect of long-term destabilization of the Middle East. Felix was a passionate Zionist and introduced this issue into their walks. Finally, one day, there was a loss of temper on both sides and a good many hard words said. That evening Dad called Felix at home and spoke to this effect: "Felix, I apologize for losing my temper, but not for my views, which remain unchanged. I suggest we forget this conversation and that we continue our walks but agree never to mention Zionism or Palestine again." And so it was agreed. This conversational island was scrupulously avoided by both men for the rest of their joint lives.

A number of Dad's Washington friends came to know F.F. Some took to him, some did not. Those who did not tended to be those who did not share his tastes and interests, those who were intimidated by his intellectual power, and those who felt that Felix monopolized the conversation time, a view with which a fair mind could agree. One who found Felix a truly kindred spirit was Wilmarth S. Lewis ("Lefty" to nearly everyone). Lewis had formidable scholarly credentials of his own from his exhaustive, lifelong immersion in the correspondence of Horace Walpole. Lefty was quick and bright, knew at least as much about English letters as Felix did, and loved gossip. Lefty had a keen and mischievous sense of humor. All of these assets were shields against any sense of intimidation.

Lefty moved to Washington to do government work during World War II. It was inevitable that he and F.F. would meet, even inevitable that they would meet at Dad's house, as they did one night at dinner. The talk turned to books, then to a particular book that seemingly had made a deep impression on Felix. Away went Felix, the conversational bit firmly in his teeth. Something he said jarred Lefty, who sought to dissent but could not intervene. Then another comment about the book jarred Lefty and a sly thought crept into Lefty's mind. He rapped on a glass. F.F.'s flow of words stopped abruptly. "Mr. Justice," said Lefty, "have you read this book?" Felix started off again: "Only a person who missed the book's point could ask that question." Lefty: "Mr. Justice, my question can be answered yes or no." The answer turned out to be no.

From then on, Lefty and Felix were fast friends. Once, lunching at F.F.'s chambers, Lefty stole a notepad stamped: "From the Chambers of Associate Justice Felix Frankfurter." Lefty used it to write notes to Felix, seeking a reaction. The latter, knowing how Lefty's mind worked, decided to ignore the purloined stationery. Finally the notes stopped. Felix, surmising that the pad was exhausted, sent Lefty a new one, without comment. Dad wrote of this to Philip Jessup: "Thus do great jurists and scholars amuse themselves."*

Frankfurter had no hobbies but his work, reading, and a voluminous correspondence. It is unlikely that he ever owned

*Letter to Philip C. Jessup, Aug. 11, 1971, *Among Friends,* p. 329.

any item of sporting equipment, or was ever in a swimming pool or ocean. Eventually, the unremitting warfare with Associate Justices Black and Douglas brought cumulative stress, and he became increasingly bitter and querulous. He had no outlets or interests to relieve the strain. By then his wife had become a severe, irreversible hypochondriac, so that his domestic circumstances added to the strain. By the time his judicial service was ended by a stroke, the fun had gone out of him. His death left Dad truly bereaved, so close had their interests and interactions become. As Dad wrote to Erwin Griswold (then Dean of the Harvard Law School): " . . . I find it hard to realize that it is all over. Almost every day something happens which I immediately remind myself to tell Felix about."*

While I would not wish to overstate Frankfurter's influence on my own life, he kindly took an interest in my legal education, particularly in steering me to the Harvard Law School. While I was there, he sometimes pressed me for candid observations on the leading figures of the faculty who overlapped his time and my own: Thomas Reed Powell, Warren Seavey, Austin W. Scott, W. Barton Leach, Roscoe Pound. In 1961 F.F. administered to me, in his chambers, my oath of office as United States Attorney for the District of Columbia. He had served as Assistant United States Attorney for the Southern District of New York under a landmark United States Attorney, Henry L. Stimson (later Taft's and F.D.R.'s Secretary of War and Hoover's Secretary of State). Felix's remarks at my swearing in made a deep impression on me: "Always remember that you carry a great power to ruin people's lives and liveli-

*Letter to Erwin Griswold, March 22, 1965, *Among Friends,* p. 266.

hoods and exercise that power with care and conscience." This was useful advice when I was confronted by certain criminal referrals from agencies interested in running up indictment statistics. His largeness of view came, no doubt, from Holmes and Stimson and was a well worth drinking from.

A Minor Miracle

I T WAS MAY OF 1948. My wife and I were planning to
have our daughter, Eleanor, christened at Christ Church,
Cambridge. We were stymied by an ordinarily innocu-
ous requirement, that we present our marriage certificate. We
could not find it.

I called Dad at his law office and soon got him on the line.
"Dad, I hate to bother you, but we can't arrange Eldie's chris-
tening without our marriage certificate, which we can't find.
We wondered if you might have it."

"Why would I have it?" said Dad.

"You were best man at our wedding."

Dad must have sensed an adversary situation in the offing,
for a defensive edge crept into his voice. "Look, if you can't
keep track of your papers, I sympathize, but don't drag me into
it. I don't think I ever had the blasted thing."

I retreated, puzzled and unconvinced, but lacking evidence
with which to press my case.

A few days later, my wife and I were entertaining old
friends at dinner in our Cambridge apartment and catching up
on several years' worth of developments in our respective lives.

They were eager to see our wedding pictures. As we turned the pages, joking about the cast of characters, we came on a striking photograph of Dad coming out of St. Bartholomew's Chapel in New York, where our marriage service had taken place. He was attired as best man, in cutaway coat, pearl gray vest, striped trousers, highly polished black shoes, wearing a smile of expansive geniality. His mustache struck an attitude

Dean Acheson with the missing marriage certificate—"A minor miracle." His companions are John and Dorothea Castles, the author's parents-in-law.

between insouciant and arrogant. There was an arresting detail. In one hand he carried a white paper envelope, which looked to be about 8 by 10 inches. In the same instant my wife and I said, "The marriage certificate!"

Within days, Dad was confronted with the photographic evidence. His response was an attitude of resignation. His highly capable and organized assistant, Barbara Evans, was called upon. "Barbara, we're both in trouble. I've been accused of larceny and am changing my plea from not guilty to guilty. But *you* are going to have to find the marriage certificate. Good luck!"

In a few minutes Barbara returned with the talisman in hand. "Where on earth did you find it?" asked Dad. "In the file," said Barbara, "under Acheson, David C., Marriage, 1943."

Dad received this miracle in a spirit of acceptance, but not of understanding. "Well, I'll be damned," he said.

Barn Burner

I T'S TIME to tear down the old barn," said Dad, "before it falls down."

There was much truth to this. The barn, well over a century old, had a rugged enough frame, some parts of which were 12″ x 12″ beams fastened with pegs and capable of supporting loads of several tons. But the sheathing was decaying badly, whole boards were missing, and every side was far from weatherproof.

Now, in the late 1950s, Dad was in the grip of what we called his "Italian period." Mother and he had made several trips to Lake Como with their Dutch friends, Mr. and Mrs. Dirk Stikker. Dirk Stikker had been Foreign Minister of the Netherlands when Dad was his American counterpart, and they had formed a firm friendship based upon mutual trust and a common enjoyment of a good time. Dad had gone so far as to tackle the Italian language with the help of language records, but finally foundered on what he called "my incurable Anglo-Saxon ear."

The barn figured in the Italianization of Dad's life through a resourceful plan. The barn's foundation was a stout, three-sided stone wall eight or nine feet high. If the timbers were pulled down, the area within the foundation was large enough to build an Italian garden with espalier trees and a large, one-story studio for Mother. The garden would be enclosed on three sides by the foundation and the studio, while two of the four walls of the studio would be the old foundation. It was a neat concept.

Inquiry was made of a local contractor, who agreed to pull down the barn and haul the lumber away for $3,000. A blueprint of the proposed studio was developed and all was ready to go forward. It was now late summer, and Mother and Dad had planned a visit to Martha's Vineyard, postponing the start of work until their return. A force from offstage, however, was to affect these plans with bizarre effect.

By an arrangement of many years standing, Dad leased most of his field acreage to a neighboring farmer, who planted it with crops of his own choice, sold his crops for his own account, and paid Dad enough rent to cover property taxes. This arrangement spared Dad the cost and bother of active farming. As part of the deal, the farmer was allowed to use Dad's barn for crop storage. As Mother and Dad were about to travel to Martha's Vineyard, it was harvest time, when wheat was cut and threshed, a predictable occurrence to which neither of them gave much thought, and off they went.

On threshing day, the sky threatened rain, and the farmer moved the threshing machine inside to the central floor of the barn. It was a gasoline-fueled machine powered by a two-cycle engine, prone to backfiring. As the farmer fed the machine with newly cut wheat, the chaff accumulated on the floor. A backfire and spark were all it took to ignite the chaff. In so short a time that the machine could not be moved, the chaff and barn were gone, and the threshing machine an iron skeleton.

When Mother and Dad returned from their trip, the barn disaster was thoroughly investigated. It developed that the barn was insured for $2,000. The fire had saved Dad the $3,000 demolition expense and put $2,000 in his pocket. He was $5,000 ahead. This put him a good leg up on the new studio building. The stone foundation was still standing and required remortaring, but was otherwise unharmed. To say that Dad was pleased by this turn of events would be a significant understatement. We cautioned him against any unseemly show of glee until the insurance proceeds were in hand, but it was not in him to dissemble. "Listen," he said, "I was in another state when the deed was done, and the only participant had every reason to want the barn saved. What a break!"

And that was as close to an expression of regret as we could get out of him.

"Just as the Twig Is Bent"*

D AD'S INTEREST IN his children's education was considerable, for a parent of his generation. Our childhood and early youth were in times when many parents let their children's schools worry about education and let the nanny raise the child. But we were fortunate in having parents both of whom were college graduates or better, and both were themselves children of parents who had taken a keen interest in *their* education.

Each summer in the country we had an organized plan of reading, plus lessons in French, piano, and other forms of self-improvement. These were pursued with grim determination in the presence of far more entertaining distractions: riding, fishing, tennis, swimming. For a time Mother and Dad, in alternation, read aloud to the plenary family group, with mixed results. This could produce thrills and chills if the menu was *Cursed Be the Treasure* or *Treasure Island,* but some of the lengthy works

*" 'Tis education forms the common mind: / Just as the twig is bent the tree's inclined"—Alexander Pope, *Moral Essays; Epistle I,* line 149.

of George Meredith found us yawning and glassy-eyed. We learned that literary taste cannot be acquired by the pound.

Shakespeare was an early favorite. Dad particularly loved the chronicle of King Henry VIII, and found poignant the tragedy there told of the ambitious Cardinal Wolsey, who rose to great heights of power by royal favor of that king, only to be broken when he presumed too far. Often Dad gave us assignments to memorize that we were to recite at the end of the day on his return home. Dad, who served briefly and thanklessly as Under Secretary of the Treasury, thought Wolsey's case exceptionally instructive for young people who might be impressed with persons of high rank in Washington. One assignment to memorize that sticks particularly in the mind was Wolsey's heart-broken lament:

> Farewell! a long farewell, to all my greatness!
> This is the state of man: to-day he puts forth
> The tender leaves of hopes; to-morrow blossoms,
> And bears his blushing honours thick upon him;
> The third day comes a frost, a killing frost,
> And, when he thinks, good easy man, full surely
> His greatness is a-ripening, nips his root,
> And then he falls, as I do. I have ventur'd,
> Like little wanton boys that swim on bladders,
> This many summers in a sea of glory,
> But far beyond my depth: my high-blown pride
> At length broke under me, and now has left me,
> Weary and old with service, to the mercy
> Of a rude stream, that must for ever hide me.
> Vain pomp and glory of this world, I hate ye!
> I feel my heart new open'd. O! how wretched
> Is that poor man that hangs on princes' favours!
> There is, betwixt that smile we would aspire to,
> That sweet aspect of princes, and their ruin,

> More pangs and fears than wars or women have—
> And when he falls, he falls like Lucifer,
> Never to hope again.
>
> —*King Henry VIII,* Act III, Sc. 2

To Dad, this was a cautionary tale for Washington political life, and he took care that his children did not miss the point.

Choices of schools developed in what appeared a natural way. Eugene Meyer, an investment banker who bought *The Washington Post,* was a friend of Dad's and a benefactor of the Madeira School in Virginia. Mr. Meyer had arranged for Dad to help the school with some legal matters and induced him to join the Board of Trustees. It seemed natural, then, that my sisters went there for a time. One sister was sent on to the Westover School, founded by the aunt of Dad's close friend, Archibald MacLeish, whose wife also went there. It seemed foreordained that an Acheson should enroll at Westover. Indeed, it was there that I met my future wife.

When I was seen as needing a firm institutional environment, it did not occur to me that it would be any but Dad's school, Groton. So off I went, prepared by a visit that Dad and I paid in the spring of 1935 in the company of George Rublee, Dad's law partner and Groton's first graduate (1886). It was not until some years later that I learned that Dad had had a poor time as a student at Groton. The founder, Endicott Peabody, found Dad rebellious and troublesome, and elsewhere in these pages is described his near dismissal from the school. Dad himself has written, somewhat elliptically, about his feelings for Groton:

. . . The organization of boarding school, like the wolf in Icelandic saga which ran up the sky and devoured the sun, devoured my early freedom. School life was organized from the wakening bell to the policed silence which followed lights-out. All was organized—eating, studying, games, so-called free time, the whole thing. One could understand and accept rendering unto Caesar the things which were Caesar's, the control of one's external life. The mind and spirit were not Caesar's; yet these were demanded, too. And I, for one, found it necessary to erect defenses of the last citadel of spiritual freedom.*

When I learned Dad's feelings about Groton, years afterward, I expressed wonder that he had sent me there, and received a somewhat dusty answer. Seemingly, it had appeared to Dad that I stood in need of just those iron qualities of tutelage that had so alienated him. No matter; I enjoyed all but my first year, and found that beneath the titular dictatorship of the old Rector and the Bismarckian authority symbol that legend had built around him there was an able and reasonably innovative faculty, some flexibility in the curriculum and in the athletic program, and some fun to be had. In my last year I took a private tutorial in Greek literature. For two hours every Saturday I met with my faculty tutor, a breezy, humorous man, also the baseball coach, and we read Euripides' *Medea* and Sophocles' *Oedipus Rex* in the original Greek. My tutor, Bill Cushing, made a deal. If we could get ahead by two Saturday periods, come the opening of pheasant season in late fall, we could spend two Saturday periods hunting pheasant in New Hampshire. With that inducement it was easy work to gain on our schedule and, as promised, we spent two Saturday afternoons hunting pheasant with Mr. Cushing's half-blind setter and an ancient 20-gauge shotgun. It was amazing how much play there was in the joints of an institution that still had a reputa-

*Morning and Noon, p. 24.

tion for strictness and regimentation. Dad found it hard to believe these tales and, I suspect, resented yet rejoiced in this belated mellowing of the school that he had found so oppressive.

Dad tended to develop fierce enthusiasms for recent discoveries, and none more than literary discoveries. In the early 1930s, he returned from New York on the train with a major find. His seat companion had been Hugh Lofting, the author of the Dr. Dolittle stories. Dad was much taken with Lofting and the universe of the imagination that Lofting had created and peopled with such strange, yet satisfying, creatures. In a few days a comprehensive Dr. Dolittle library was acquired. All of us read these volumes exhaustively. *The Voyages of Dr. Dolittle,* with its incomparable account of Spidermonkey Island, must rank with great travel literature, for all its fantasy.

Similarly, but at a later time, Dad discovered Vernon Louis Parrington's *Main Currents of American Thought.* This I was to read in toto, as Dad did. Mentioned there, and particularly attractive to us, were some works of antebellum novelists who wrote of the old South and of the border states when the western frontier was in Kentucky and Tennessee. The stand-outs were Augustus Longstreet's *Georgia Scenes,* Charleston's William Gilmore Simms, author of *The Forayers* and *Woodcraft,* Joseph G. Baldwin with his *Flush Times of Alabama and Mississippi,* and Robert Montgomery Bird's *Nick of the Woods,* the latter a blood and thunder tale of a ruthless Indian fighter who evened the score against the marauding red man. While this work would hardly pass the test of "political correctness" today, it was deeply satisfying to the young grandson of a former Indian fighter. The other works mentioned were rugged,

colorful contemporary tales of the deep South before the senti-
mental post-bellum writers transformed it to a Spanish moss-
covered romance of the Lost Cause, mannered aristocrats, and
debts of honor. These earlier writers dealt with card sharks,
knife fighters, crack shots, hard-riding bucks, and women who
could break a horse and manage a plantation.

A critical contribution that Dad made in bending the twig
of my education occurred in the summer of 1939, as I was
admitted to Yale and was planning my courses. The coming of
war was obvious to Dad, as was the eventual involvement of
the United States. He urged me to enroll in the Army or Navy
ROTC—Yale had both. This made eminent sense to me, but
which? The Army ROTC was training for the artillery arm,
while the Navy ROTC was general training in navigation and
engineering, holding out a vague but discernible promise of
service on ships. I liked boats and the sea, and so the choice was
made which opened up one of the most valuable experiences of
my life. Dad's bet on war was right on the money.

Dad always felt that the highest use of his time, next to
getting education, was to give it. This value led him to divert
energy in his later life to speak to student audiences at Groton
and St. Paul's schools, at Yale, at King's College, Cambridge,
the U.S. Military Academy at West Point, the Air War College, and other places of learning too numerous to catalogue.
He did not do this from any desire to teach orthodoxy, to put
students on the true path of belief, but to acquaint them with a
world of events, issues, and dimensions of which, otherwise,
they might never learn. What he wanted to convey was not just
factual history, but what it was to be there, to have to cope. He
wished to convey what the historian C. V. Wedgwood spoke

Leading the academic procession of Harvard University's 299th commencement: Dean Acheson and Archibald MacLeish. ACME PHOTO

of: "History is lived forwards but it is written in retrospect. We know the end before we consider the beginning and we can never wholly recapture what it was to know the beginning only."*

It was "the beginning only" that Dad wished to recapture for his youthful audiences. It was that purpose that lay behind his use of the title *Present at the Creation* for his memoirs.

Dad was too human not to relish the role of educator for its frequent spice of flattery. As he wrote to Wilmarth Lewis in 1958:

My days at Cambridge are already half gone. They have been a delight. . . . Cambridge has been wonderfully warm and hospitable to me. And how right you were to urge me to come along. . . . And, then, I am flattered into euphoria—my lectures are packed, with people on the floor, and in the aisles, and another lecture room with a loudspeaker for the overflow. . . . One of the sterner dons told me that I was lucky to be lecturing at the beginning of the year. "The new men," he said, "haven't caught on yet, and go to lectures."†

But Dad's interest in exciting younger minds was not limited to organized or advanced audiences. Once, when Dad was Secretary of State, the young (age eleven) son of close friends had been through a rough time with a serious illness and Dad thought of a way to attach the boy's mind to a new and arresting point of focus. He invited the convalescent to lunch in the Secretary's private dining room, and sent the Secretary's driver to pick the boy up at home. Dad turned up all the theatrical

*C. V. Wedgwood, *William the Silent* (London: Jonathan Cape, 1967), pp. 35 and 212.

†Letter to Wilmarth S. Lewis, undated (written from King's College in September 1958), *Among Friends*, p. 143.

touches to full throttle. His young guest was put at ease by the fatherly and considerate driver and, as they approached the Department of State garage, the driver turned on the siren. Steel doors rose to admit the young VIP, who was taken up in the private elevator. Dad greeted him as a valued guest who was gracious enough to give Dad some time, and the two had an animated and informal lunch. Dad then swore his guest to secrecy and brought in the Department's Director of Intelligence and Research, who took them through the recent cables and a briefing on the progress of the war in Korea. Then the guest was driven home, resolutely declining to reveal to his family the briefing, the conversation, even the menu. Thus, a young American had tasted the sense, in Wedgwood's phrase, of "what it was to know the beginning only."

Dad's interest in the education of the young was fully reflected in his enthusiasm for the education of his grandchildren. He encouraged his granddaughter Eleanor's decision to go to law school, and enjoyed discussing with her issues of the day to which she applied a keen and critical mind. He agreed to speak at his grandson David's graduation from Phillips Exeter Academy, where young David helped him out of an awkward box aggravated by the recent assassination of Robert F. Kennedy, which Dad described in a letter:

. . . Mr. Day, the Yale Principal of the school, told me that some of the more excitable of the seniors had started a plan to walk out as one on the theory that I was a "hawk" on Vietnam. He very wisely asked them to document their statement which they, of course, could not do. Then Dave undertook to meet the ring leaders and give them a sketch of my views over the years which surprised them a good deal.

The speech made a great hit with the parents. Perhaps the "malcontents" wished they had walked out after all.*

When Dad's grandson Peter was almost twelve years old (1966), Dad was hard at work on his memoirs of his State Department service. My wife and I and our three children were invited to lunch at the farm on a weekend. When we arrived, we sensed a palpable suspense in the air. Something was afoot. At lunch Dad revealed his surprise, wearing an expression of great self-satisfaction.

"Well, I've chosen a title for my memoirs. It will be *Present at the Creation.* I don't suppose any of you could guess where that comes from?"

"Sure," said Peter. "It comes from Alfonso the Learned, King of Spain, who said, 'Had I been present at the creation, I would have given some useful hints for the better ordering of the universe.' "

Dad had the grace to say, "Good for you," but he looked like a child whose toy has been snatched from him. Later he whispered to Eleanor, indicating Peter: "Don't pet him. He bites."

*Letter to J. H. P. Gould, June 11, 1968, *Among Friends,* p. 299.

Values

MOST OF DAD'S ATTACHMENTS and aversions came from his basic values. These, in no particular order, were: fairness, honesty, loyalty, order, service, realism, and enjoyment of work and life. He admired and felt affection for people who shared and lived these values, and had the reverse of those feelings for people who did not live and share them. This was the key to his coolness toward F.D.R. and his devotion to Harry Truman.

Dad did not like slick people, lobbyists, finaglers. His greatest contempt was for people who put their own career or material interests ahead of obligations, and Washington was (and is) full of them. He had little use for people who took government positions for a year or two for the notoriety, or to generate clients, as many lawyers did and do. In military people he often found the admirable qualities of loyalty and straightforwardness and the basis for trust and friendship—Harry Leonard (a retired Marine officer with one arm), Raymond E. Lee (an Army officer, at one time U.S. military attaché at the London embassy), Alan G. Kirk (a naval officer who commanded the Allied task force at the Normandy landings on D-Day, 1944),

Alice Acheson adjusts Dean Acheson's decoration as General Omar Bradley
looks on. CAPITAL PRESS SERVICE

George C. Marshall (a five-star general and Chief of Staff, U.S.
Army, during World War II, the "architect of victory," later
Secretary of State and Secretary of Defense), Matthew Ridg-
way (a four-star general who commanded the U.S. military
recovery during the Korean War), and Omar Bradley (a general
commanding 12th Army Group in Europe in World War II,
later Chief of Staff, U.S. Army, and a five-star general).

Journalists rarely met these requirements for Dad, particularly after he came into official positions. There were many
whose company he enjoyed, who were witty, full of interesting
gossip, and could provide an entertaining evening, but he knew
that their interest in him was to reach across his lowered guard
for a story. More than once he remarked of a journalist: "I'm

Dean to him, but he would give his right arm for a story about my indictment." Dad had considerable disdain for *The Washington Post* for what he saw as editorial positions leaning to pious conventional wisdom and a reportorial preoccupation with prying and tendentious details about personalities, or "who struck John?" A particular disenchantment with journalists that stuck in Dad's mind stemmed from the role played by the press in magnifying Senator Joseph McCarthy's irresponsible charges of Communist subversion in the State Department. In Dad's view, Senator McCarthy was the evil instigator, but journalists were his eager accomplices.

Two chief anti-values in Dad's declension were parochial thinking and conventional wisdom. Parochialism was to him the anti-value of long-term realism. An example comes to mind. When the Iranian government of Mossadegh seized the assets of an Anglo-Iranian Oil Company in 1951, Secretary Acheson sought to work out a consortium for the sale of oil produced by those assets, believing that economic and political stability in Iran would thus be served and that would be the necessary predicate to restoring relations between Iran and the West. The British, Dad was convinced, had lost sight of long-range issues and had become obsessed with recovery of AIOC assets at any cost. This was the first major loss of confidence in the reliability of the British that fractured Dad's former high regard for that country and government. The second was the disastrous British misjudgment of the possible success of the attack on Suez in 1956. Thereafter, Dad was no longer an Anglophile. The British, in his view, had abandoned the value of realism.

The realist in Dad was always tickled by Chancellor

Adenauer's, "Der Alte's," sardonic view of the world. Dad reported to me a meeting with the old chancellor in the 1960s in Germany on an occasion spent in reminiscences and lawn bowling. The conversation turned to the prospects for economic unification of western Europe. Dad asked: "Chancellor, who do you think will be the greater man in history, Schuman or de Gaulle?" Adenauer replied without hesitation: "De Gaulle." Dad: "Now you surprise me, Chancellor. You and Schuman have been the strong friends of European union, de Gaulle its bitter enemy. I should think you would put Schuman ahead of de Gaulle." "But you must see," said the chancellor, "that de Gaulle will outlive Schuman and he will write the history himself." And, indeed, so it came to pass.

Anti-value number two in Dad's declension was conventional wisdom. He felt that there was always a shallow, but commonly accepted, way of thinking about a given issue, a current political fashion, usually associated with some noble aspiration to which careerists would attach themselves and which would regularly appear in the Washington press. It was a mark of timidity. Today, we would call this "intellectual chic" or "political correctness." One of Dad's prize examples was the way independence for the African colonies of Europe had become not only a tenet of U.S. foreign policy, but an uncritical faith of nearly universal acceptance. He could easily see that maybe colonies could not be retained and defended as a matter of power, but there could be no reasonable belief in multiplying parliamentary democracies in the colonial areas. Dad believed in evidence. He was impressed by the history of tribal warfare in nearly every sub-Sahara country and the overlapping of irrational national borders by numerous tribes. He knew, of course,

that American politicians did not wish to face these facts. By
the time of Dad's death, there might have been as many as two
former African colonies that did *not* have one-party dictatorship government dominated by the hegemonic tribe. Many
of these systematically pillaged the public treasury, conducted
genocide against other tribes, and generally made a mockery of
any notion of democracy. All of this saddened Dad, but did not
surprise him.

Dad was skeptical of the notion of peacetime inspirational
leadership. He believed in sagacious, steady, far-sighted leaders
and leadership. He felt that General Marshall exemplified
these values. He had a profound admiration for Baron Manner-
heim, the father and three times savior of modern Finland, for
his unique steadfastness in the face of seemingly insuperable
obstacles. For reasons consistent with these values Dad liked to
read biography, collections of letters, and diaries of statesmen,
chiefly British and American of the eighteenth and nineteenth
centuries. To him it was important to know not merely what
happened but who made it happen, how the participants
managed events and how they coped with events they could
not manage. When he was Secretary of State he found that his
reading of history and biography enabled him to see his problems in a comforting perspective compared with other and
more trying times in history.

Dad knew that, as a statesman, he could only work at the
margin of the larger forces in foreign affairs. He had humility,
not in the sense of self-effacement, but an accurate sense of his
secondary place in the universe. If he thought of himself as a
leader at all, it was with Justice Holmes's metaphor in mind:

"We lead," wrote Holmes, "in the same sense that small

boys lead a circus parade when they march ahead of it. But if they turn down a side street the parade goes on."

Edward B. Burling, Dad's senior law partner, wrote to him in 1954 of an introduction Dad had written for a friend's book:

You are becoming the author of a definite creed, a sound one. Most affairs—especially foreign affairs—are complicated. There is no easy answer. They can never really be "solved." But you can do something about them. In truth, you should do something about them right along. But they will always be with us. They are like the state of your liver, or the weather, or other things that we have with us all the time and that, all the time, we have to do something about.*

Dad was a skeptic; that is to say, he distinguished between hope and illusion. He believed thoughtful application could accomplish useful things. He did not look for dramatic breakthroughs. He had a profound suspicion of statesmen who thought of themselves as Atlas shouldering the burdens of the world. He never thought of himself as constructing anything as pretentious as "world order" and distrusted self-dramatization that enabled the mind to take such a concept seriously. He believed in aims as the intellectual framework of policy, but those aims must be identifiable, concrete. He insisted that statecraft must be guided and informed by those objectives. He often used Andrew Jackson's command (perhaps apocryphal) at the Battle of New Orleans as an antidote to abstract, pretentious thought: "Elevate them guns a little lower."

The passage of time seemed to Dad to make political leaders less prone to think about problems to be solved and more prone to preoccupy themselves with, as he put it, "the political

*Undated note from Edward B. Burling to Dean Acheson (surely in 1950s).

198

reflection of the problems." The obsession with "image" seemed to Dad to be a fatal, weakening disability. In a letter to Harry Truman in the 1960s, he wrote about "image—that dreadful word," as the obsession of the Kennedy administration, using the metaphor of a baseball player's first thought when he hears the crack of the bat: "How am I going to look fielding this hot line drive to second base? A good way to miss the ball altogether."*

Occasionally, romantic indiscretions of his acquaintances prompted Dad to share his view of marital infidelities: infidelities were breaches of loyalty, they worked unfairly, they were dishonest, they attacked order, they were usually based on unrealistic judgment. These were essentially objections of policy rather than of morality. The transgressor thus forfeited his or her claim to be regarded as a person of responsibility or trustworthiness.

To Dad, loyalty ran down as well as up. His staff, whether younger lawyers or State Department officials, were intensely loyal to him and he returned that loyalty in full measure. An employee who earned his loyalty could count on it thereafter. A vivid example comes to mind. In the late 1950s one of the Hill family at Sandy Spring, who had long worked for and with Dad on farm chores (we will call him "B"), was arrested by the Montgomery County police on a Saturday night for speeding and was charged with drunk driving. (There were circumstances that led Dad to believe the charges might be true.) B was held until Monday morning court, but called Dad from the station. Dad agreed to appear as his counsel. On Monday

*Letter to Harry Truman, July 14, 1961, *Among Friends*, p. 208.

morning a somewhat worse-for-wear B, in custody, met Dad in court in Rockville, Maryland, the county seat. The charges were read and the charging officer testified. On cross examination Dad asked the officer if a breath analysis, blood analysis, or urinalysis had been run on B after arrest. No. Was there a bottle or other physical evidence of liquor in the car? No. What was the evidence supporting the charge of drunk driving? The smell of whiskey on the breath of the accused. Wouldn't a single drink be enough to put the smell of whiskey on the breath of the accused? It might be. Did the officer have a radar instrument to measure the accused's speed? No, he did not. Did he make any contemporaneous notes? No, he did not. What was the evidence of speeding? The accused's car was weaving. Did the officer have to speed to overtake the accused? No, the accused had slowed when the siren and flashing light went on.

Dad addressed the magistrate: "Your honor, I move to dismiss the charges on the strength of the arresting officer's own testimony." The county prosecutor stepped forward. "Your honor, I move that the charge be amended to operating a vehicle without due care and attention, as the weaving evidence shows." Dad became somber. "Your honor, up until now I had supposed this to be the Free State of Maryland, but after hearing the prosecutor I wonder if I am in the Soviet Union where charges can be manipulated at will by the state." The magistrate spoke for the first time: "Case dismissed."

That afternoon B came around to the farm and sought Dad out. "Mr. Acheson, I can't afford much of a fee, but I have something here that might do." He pulled from his coat pocket a flat pint of Wild Turkey Bourbon. "I have no thought of any fee, B, but I will accept your present and join you in a toast to the Free State of Maryland." Which he did.

Dad despised his successor as Secretary of State, John Foster Dulles, for what Dad saw as a callous absence of loyalty to the professional employees of the department, bespeaking absence of loyalty in his character. Early in Dulles's tenure, Dulles admonished the employees that he expected "positive loyalty" of them. This was taken as an ellipticism for requiring that the considerable attachment of the staff to Acheson be transferred to Dulles. Apart from the pettiness that Dad saw in this gesture, it soon became clear that Dulles was not prepared to earn the loyalty of the staff by loyalty to them. This was confirmed by Dulles's dismissal of a number of outstanding officers for their personification of politically unpopular (in Republican circles) views. Some of these officers had had the backbone to report the eroding position of Chiang Kai-shek's rule of China in realistic and accurate terms, an inexcusable heresy. Others were the targets of trumped-up charges of disloyalty or Communist sympathy leveled by Senator Joseph McCarthy and other "primitives," as Dad called them. These human sacrifices did not appear to trouble Dulles and outraged Dad, who thought it a great arrogance that Dulles could imagine loyalty as running only to himself. Dad came to agree fully with the view expressed in Harold Macmillan's memoirs, that Dulles was untrustworthy.

Dad hated a fuss. An open show of personal resentment or a temper tantrum of any kind, or outbursts of tears of self-pity, made him uncomfortable and irritated. These things were selfish, undisciplined, disorderly. There were a lot of unpleasant things in life that one must put up with; best to do it quietly and/or effectively as possible, without demoralizing the women and children. This attitude came directly from his father, a clergyman and erstwhile soldier. Moreover, Dad did not like gratuitous clatter—interruptions, unnecessary raising of voices, bickering and pointless recrimination. He became impatient at the fussing of children and regarded highly the duty of parents to keep children inaudible. A word of high pejorative value in Dad's declension was "contretemps," denoting a brouhaha, a "rhubarb," order and quiet breaking down.

In A. Whitney Griswold, president of Yale from 1950 to 1962, Dad found a truly kindred spirit. Values that they shared included devotion to Yale (Dad had been a member of the Yale Corporation since 1936), a lively sense of fun and entertainment, a high degree of social conviviality, and an instinct for innovation. Dad had identified these qualities in Griswold when the latter was a professor in the Yale government department, and their friendship blossomed during the late 1930s and the 1940s. When President Charles Seymour retired, Dad was determined to bring Griswold to the presidency. The perceived obstacle was Senator Robert A. Taft of Ohio, also a member of the Yale Corporation, who was thought to distrust Griswold's lack of reverence for established ways of doing things and to see in him a potential Acheson ally—a strong negative presumption in the mind of an isolationist Republican.

Now Dad's innovative spirit came into play. A scheme would have to be devised which would bring Taft into camp. The mechanism employed was what today would be called the "good cop, bad cop" routine. The "bad cop" was to be Wilmarth S. Lewis, a Yale Corporation colleague and Dad's close friend, with a similar bent for elaborate conspiracy. The plot

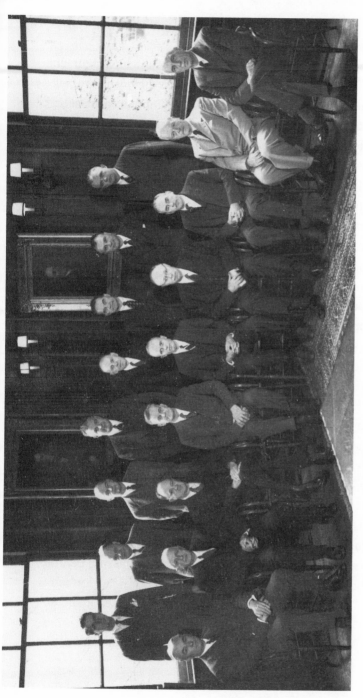

Dean Acheson at a 1950 Yale Corporation meeting shortly before he was sworn in as Secretary of State. In seeking to bring in A. Whitney Griswold as President Seymour's successor, Acheson had to outmaneuver Senator Robert A. Taft.

President A. Whitney Griswold (*center, front*); Dean Acheson (*front row, second on Griswold's left*); Senator Robert A. Taft (first on Griswold's left); Wilmarth S. Lewis (end of front row, on Griswold's right). YALE UNIVERSITY LIBRARY, MANUSCRIPTS AND ARCHIVES

that they hatched was clever. Lewis, a full-time litterateur, collector, and editor of the correspondence of Horace Walpole, was well equipped to play the role of the impractical armchair intellectual and, so cast, he undertook to propose a radical candidate for the presidency. It had to be someone who would horrify Taft but was of sufficient stature to seem a serious threat. Dad and Lewis selected Robert M. Hutchins to be the unwitting human bait; he was then president of the University of Chicago and the proponent of the "Great Books" program of education. He had been Dean of the Yale Law School, which polished his plausibility as a decoy. Lewis put Hutchins's name forward. Taft was horrified, as both conspirators hoped and expected. In a Corporation meeting Dad indicated qualified support for Hutchins, made a show of being on the fence, but fell back on a speech urging a more mainstream educator, someone perhaps like Whitney Griswold. Dad privately indicated to Taft that if Griswold were not accepted by the Corporation, Dad would see merit in Lewis's support for Hutchins.

The Senator from Ohio was in a box familiar to many senators—go along with the lesser of two evils. Dad's candidate stirred Taft's suspicion, but Lewis's candidate excited his fright. Griswold was duly elected with Taft's support.

Dad was as pleased as a small boy by the neatness of this maneuver. Everything had come together with a click. Yale had benefited. Griswold had benefited. No one was hurt. The only loose end was Lefty Lewis's discomfort at playing the role of advocate for the straw man. He reminded Dad for some time to come that Dad's debt to him would not easily be expunged.

It did not take Dad long to come to a sense of Harry Tru-

Dean Acheson and Harry S. Truman, 1955. ELLIS PHOTO

man's character and reliability. Within two weeks of the death of President Roosevelt, Dad wrote:

> . . . It so happened that two days before the President's death, I had a long meeting with Mr. Truman and for the first time got a definite impression. It was a very good impression. He is straightforward, decisive, simple, entirely honest. He, of course, has the limitations upon his judgment and wisdom that the limitations of his experiences produce, but I think that he will learn fast and will inspire confidence. It seems to me a blessing that he is the President and not Henry Wallace.* I am afraid that we would have been plunged into bitter partisan rowing under Henry Wallace. I listened to him testify

*Wallace had been Vice President in Roosevelt's third term (1941–45).

the other day on our trade agreements bill and got, in a few minutes, a complete demonstration of how his weak points completely destroy his strong ones. He was well informed and gave excellent testimony. However, on two or three occasions hostile questions made him quite lose his temper, whereupon he made some ill-considered remarks and the whole hearing turned into a brawl.*

In his memoir *Morning and Noon,* Dad contrasted his sense of Mr. Truman with his feelings about President Roosevelt:

The impressions given me by President Roosevelt carried much of this attitude of European—not British—royalty. The latter is comfortably respectable, dignified, and bourgeois. The President could relax over his poker parties and enjoy Tom Corcoran's accordion, he could and did call everyone from his valet to the Secretary of State by his first name and often made up Damon Runyon nicknames for them, too—"Tommy, the Cork," "Henry, the Morgue," and similar names; he could charm an individual or a nation. But he condescended. Many reveled in apparent admission to an inner circle. I did not—to me it was patronizing and humiliating. . . . He remained a formidable man, a leader who won admiration and respect. In others he inspired far more, affection and devotion. For me, that was reserved for a man of whom at that time I had never heard, his successor.†

As a result of his disenchanting experience in the early Roosevelt New Deal—he had been dismissed by Roosevelt as Under Secretary of the Treasury over a policy disagreement,‡

*Letter to David C. Acheson, April 30, 1945, *Present at the Creation,* p. 104.
†*Morning and Noon,* p. 165.
‡This episode is fully reported in *Morning and Noon.* F.D.R. wanted Dad, as Acting Secretary, to support the legality of the use of executive authority and funds of the Reconstruction Finance Corporation to control the price of gold, which Dad felt he could not do.

Dad returned to his law practice at the end of 1933 still a Roosevelt Democrat, but one in whom the fires of missionary enthusiasm were banked, to say the least. By the middle of President Roosevelt's second term a number of influential Democrats had withdrawn their support of Roosevelt's programs, notably Lewis W. Douglas, formerly Roosevelt's Director of the Budget, and Senators Millard E. Tydings (D.-Maryland) and Walter George (D.-Georgia). These and others were castigated as "Tories" by F.D.R., and in the congressional elections of 1938 F.D.R. sought to purge the Senate of Tydings and George by exerting pressure on the state Democratic Party nomination process. Dad's rebellious nature was ignited by what he saw as imperious bullying by F.D.R. in Dad's own state. Besides, he liked and respected Tydings. So he went to work for Tydings's renomination and reelection, and spoke in Tydings's behalf at fundraisers and voter audiences around the state. Both Tydings and George were returned to the Senate comfortably, and Dad took quiet pleasure in having a small role in teaching the "Squire of Hyde Park" something about local self-determination.

Though Dad devoted his best years (most of the period 1941 through 1952, or ages forty-eight through fifty-nine) to public service at a barely supportable financial sacrifice, it would be a mistake to think that he saw himself as a selfless martyr to his country's good. He was stimulated by public service, by the span of the issues, by the potential reach of wise decisions far beyond anything he had experienced in law practice. He liked the stretching of his capabilities that he experienced in government, and the sense that here was something

worth working for. He summarized this sense in a notable letter to a friend:

Today, more than ever before, the prize of the general is not a bigger
tent, but command. The managers of industry and finance have the
bigger tents, but command rests with government. Command, or if
one prefers, supreme leadership, demands and gives scope for the
exercise of every vital power a man has in the direction of excellence.*

Dad often counseled me and some of my friends that these
psychic rewards of public service would only come from holding substantial responsibility and were most unlikely to come
from holding junior positions where donkey work and bureau-
cratic resistance would carry much frustration. This conviction
was reinforced by advice that Justice Brandeis gave him years
earlier, that one could only serve one's country conscientiously
if one were prepared to resign on short notice, and this required
a degree of financial independence that was rarely a companion
of tender youth.

But even a position of responsibility could prove frustrating
to Dad, as he passed his fourth year as an Assistant Secretary of
State: "I am getting full of years and venom in the Department. Not giving a damn for my betters I shall probably get
fired but enjoy a freedom of expression not given to more cau-
tious officers. The Acting Secretary† gives me the most acute
pain."‡

Dad had strong views about how government should work.

*Letter to Philip H. Watts, Dec. 9, 1957, *Among Friends,* p. 132.
†The reference apparently is to Joseph Grew, though Dad came to agree
with him on the retention of the Emperor of Japan.
‡Letter to Mary A. Bundy, May 30, 1945, *Among Friends,* p. 55.

These views did not derive from *a priori* attitudes, but from experience and from a basic approach—how do we maximize the chances of making a good decision and making it stick? Generally, the answer was: make the mission clear to the administration players, to the Congress, and to the voters; assign responsibilities, make people accountable to carry them out, adduce the best objective advice on the pieces of the problem. This could be summarized in a different way: follow orderly methodology, and focus on the problem, not the political reflection or the "P.R." of the problem.

To Dad, a strong president was fundamental. But effective leadership meant straightforward leadership. One could not hide the ball from Congress or the electorate and expect support when the crunch came. Much less could one hide the ball from one's own team and expect loyalty and productive work. Where F.D.R. had set his cabinet at odds with each other and "kept them guessing," Dad favored the Truman approach—make sure that each knows his job, see that he does it, and support him when he does. To Dad the inevitable price of slyness was confusion.

A cardinal rule to Dad was "no surprises." One's chance of seeing a policy succeed was proportionate to the breadth and depth of understanding and acceptance by one's foreign allies, by the Congress, and by the voters. It was on this principle that the bipartisan foreign policy rested and for this reason that General Marshall and Dad sought to involve opposition party figures of stature and influence in the work of foreign policy, of whom Arthur Vandenberg, "Doc" Eaton, John Sherman Cooper, Paul Hoffman, and Ellsworth Bunker were exemplars, among others.* (Vandenberg was, at different times, chairman or ranking minority member of the Senate Foreign Relations Committee; Eaton was Vandenberg's counterpart in the House; Cooper was U.S. Senator from Kentucky and an adviser to Dad in several conferences abroad; Hoffman was Administrator of the Marshall Plan agency, the Economic Cooperation

*I omit here numerous distinguished Republicans who served in Washington during World War II and therefore might not be thought to qualify as opposition party figures in the postwar era.

October 1950, discussing a unified defense of Europe with French Minister of Defense M. Jules Moch (*far left*), and General of the Army George C. Marshall. NEW YORK TIMES BOOK REVIEW

Administration; Bunker was, in Dad's official life, U.S. Ambassador in Argentina and Italy.) Dad fully understood the frustration felt by Republicans at having seen Democrats in the White House since 1933. He recognized that foreign policy goals could not be realized during or after Mr. Truman's term unless responsibility was felt on both sides of the political aisle.

The gardener analogy seemed to Dad the right one. The bloom of policy was the gardener's responsibility, but not his creation. He worked at the margin of nature and must depend upon soil, sun, moisture, fertilizer, and assiduous care to optimize the growth of the bloom. With luck and work, each natural factor could be an enhancement; without luck and work, each factor could be a threat; the combination was critical.

Dad enjoyed (if that is the right word) a reputation as tough, blunt, sardonic and to-the-point, and it was well earned. He had been through a lot, he was smart, he was usually busy, and he saw little reason to let people waste his time on empty civilities. Like the first Duke of Wellington, he had a long track record of devasting rejoinders. By middle age, Dad had come to a degree of hardness of character, and had run out of patience, not with fun, but with frivolity. The "putdown" was his way of dealing with inanity and he developed it to an art form. A case comes to mind, reported to me by an immediate witness. At a press conference that Dad conducted as Secretary of State, when the question period came, a Slavic journalist propounded an argumentative, tendentious question. Dad mistook the gentleman's identity from his seating in the press room and started: "I will respond to the question, if one may call it a question, by the representative of Tass . . . " The indignant gentleman interrupted: "The Secretary should know that I do not represent Tass, but the Information Service of the People's Republic of Poland." Dad took the correction on the half-volley: "I stand corrected: Demi-Tass."

But while Dad could be as hard-shelled and blunt as anyone, he fell back on exquisite manners as a defense against puzzling challenges. Once, lunching at a restaurant by himself, he noticed a friend, a four-star admiral, come in with a much younger, beauteous blonde who was not known to Dad, but clearly not a member of the admiral's family. To Dad's consternation, the couple was shown to the adjacent table. Dad had no wish to be a witness to an indiscreet meeting nor to embarrass his friend. The admiral, on the other hand, wanted it clearly understood that his lunch was wholly above board. He sought to catch Dad's eye, which became engrossed in a newspaper. Dad finished his lunch, paid and left, walking past the admiral's table without so much as a nod. That afternoon the admiral called Dad at his office: "Dean, I want you to know I saw you and you saw me at lunch and that blonde I was with was my aide's wife, and I took her to lunch at his request to offer some advice." Dad: "Well, it's none of my business and you don't owe me any explanation. I thought a gentleman should look the other way." Admiral: "You're right, but when you're so God-damned polite about it, I know you had the wrong idea."

What did Dad, son of an Episcopal bishop, make of God? The candid answer must be: less than one might think, yet the literature and music of the church and above all the ethical frame of Christianity impressed Dad with a deep, lifelong stamp. His childhood and early youth were filled with regular church worship, both at his father's church and at Groton School, where daily chapel was compulsory. From these and from his father's example came a strong liking for church music and for hymns—which he sang in enthusiastic baritone—and an impressive familiarity with the Old and New Testaments, the Book of Common Prayer, and the epistles of St. Paul. He had no sympathy with the popular suspicion of high church style, but relished the orchestral music of religious holiday services with brasses and kettledrums.

Early in adult life Dad had come to feel that all his years of compulsory church services had put him in a permanent surplus position. When he and Mother bought their farm in Maryland in the early 1920s, Sunday was thereafter committed to the farm. Though they joined St. John's Church in Georgetown on the recommendation of close friends, it was rare that the farm was abandoned on Sunday in favor of church services. Such sacrifices usually coincided with Dad's parents' visits to Washington. On those occasions we children were dressed with appropriate decorousness and filed into St. John's Church under Dad's admonitory eye, trying against nature to suppress wiggling and whispered conversation until church was out. Dad was very attentive during the sermons, often far beyond the merit of the material. It seems to me now that he viewed the preacher as an advocate and was grading his performance, analyzing the structure of the sermon, asking himself how he would have organized a sermon focused on the same message. No doubt the preacher took Dad's steady analytical scrutiny for something less critical, for the sermons never lacked confidence.

We never heard Dad talk about God, or indeed about any theological issue. He had little or no interest in religion as such. To him, the Christian ethical values were compelling, and he talked freely about telling the truth, helping people who were in trouble, standing behind one's friends. We were frequently made aware of an acquaintance or some public figure who did not live up to these requirements and thereby forfeited Dad's respect. But the nature of God, whether He was kindly or not, what purpose He might have for mankind, were matters too opaque and remote from life to detain Dad's attention. As he grew toward middle age, and certainly when he grew older than that, he found too much evil loose in the world to have much faith in divine guidance. He sometimes quoted from *King Lear:*

> As flies to wanton boys, are we to the gods;
> They kill us for their sport.
>
> —Act IV, Sc. 1

On a few occasions the perversity of events made him feel positively atheistic, as in 1967 when President de Gaulle visited Canada and sought to stimulate Quebec separatism:

. . . Mike Pearson [former Prime Minister of Canada] writes me that de Gaulle has made problems in Canada by stirring up a matter which everyone, or almost everyone, had decided was bad medicine. Now like the press with [late Senator Joseph] McCarthy, comment and controversy have again become mutually stimulating. He would be better in the Invalides. What a wicked old fool! I find the Devil easier to believe in than God.*

One must allow here for emotional stress, perhaps.

Akin to Dad's lack of concern for the theological side of religion was his unworried contemplation of the prospect of death. When, in his autumn of life, he suffered a small stroke, from which he made a seemingly speedy recovery, his worst

*Letter to Louis Halle, Aug. 14, 1967, *Among Friends*, p. 284.

worry was a recurrence that would disable him, not kill him. He had a horror of Felix Frankfurter's end—a long decline with increasing loss of faculties and temper, a cruel reversal of his personality. Dad wished to die as the person he knew he was, not as a relic betrayed by his body. He said in his typically acerbic way: "When the time comes for me to check out, don't let the doctors be too damn diligent in holding me back." He had his wish. On Columbus Day, 1971, Death took him unawares, in seconds.

Appendix

Letter from Dean Acheson to Endicott Peabody,
Rector of Groton School, dated July 31, 1911

Dear Mr. Peabody,
This is just a line because I thought that you might be interested
to know how I was spending the summer—though it could
hardly be called summer any longer up here. I am up in North-
ern Ontario working on the new Government Railway which
Canada is building across the continent. We are just a few
hundred miles—about three—south of Hudson's Bay and right
in the heart of the "bush." Cochrane, the Port Town in North-
ern Ontario is about two hundred miles east of us, while our
camp is a thirty mile walk from the rails. Every ten miles along
the line there is a Government Residency, where an engineer
and his staff live. Where the rails are the Residencies are log
cabins but up here we live in tents. There are usually four of
these in a Residency; the office, where the Resident Engineer
and his assistant live, the bunk house where the Rodman, Tape-
man [sic], Government Timekeeper and Axeman live; the cook-

ery, and the cache where the provisions are hauled in during the winter. It is impossible to haul after the snow goes, so there have been no fresh vegetables or meat in camp since spring. You can't imagine what a luxury potatoes would be.

I was sent up to Residency 20 as axeman and then transferred after a little while to twenty-five and promoted to Timekeeper. So I shouldered my pack and walked the thirty miles in. Up here the men are just putting up the grade and cutting through the hills. The Timekeeper has to walk over his ten miles and keep track of the number of men, horses, carts, amount done, and all that sort of thing. But as we are short of men the "chief," as the engineer is called, takes me out on the surveying work. However, as both jobs can be done at once it doesn't make much more work.

This is the finest country imaginable. Half a mile from the right-of-way the country is unknown. Only the Indians have been there. Frequently an old buck will stalk into camp to trade some moose meat for salt pork. Sometimes, too, they bring their squaws, carrying their babies on their backs. A more stolid people I have never seen. I have watched the mail carrier, an Indian, during a rainy day sit for half a day at a time and never speak or even look up from his deep study of a crack in the floor.

The work runs about fifty miles further west, then comes a gap of several hundred miles to where they are working East from Lake Nepigon. You see they can only work where existing roads or navigable water makes it possible to get into the country.

I think I shall go out about the middle of September, although if the prospectors strike gravel pits on our work, as they think they will, I may not be able to get out until the rush of work is over. However, I hope they don't, as it would be very inconvenient.

Please remember me very kindly to Mrs. Peabody and Rose and Helen. I am looking forward to seeing you all very soon in Groton.

With all hopes for a pleasant voyage home, I am

Yours respectfully,
Dean Acheson